Raymond Aron

ON WAR

Translated from the French
by Terence Kilmartin

The Norton Library
W · W · NORTON & COMPANY · INC ·
NEW YORK

FOREWORD TRANSLATED BY LUCILE H. BROCKWAY

SBN 393 00107 5

PUBLISHED SIMULTANEOUSLY IN CANADA
BY GEORGE J. MCLEOD LIMITED, TORONTO

PRINTED IN THE UNITED STATES OF AMERICA

2 3 4 5 6 7 8 9 0

Foreword

THIS short book appeared eleven years ago. In a century marked by the accelerated pace of history, an author does not reread his own work after such a long interval without some anxiety, especially when it is a question of an essay on current affairs. He must resist the temptation to correct himself, to rectify a judgment refuted by subsequent events, to suppress a manifest error. At each moment he compares what he wrote with what he would write today. The reader has the right to make the same comparisons for himself. He will therefore find the text in this new edition exactly as it was set down in August 1956, before the Suez crisis and the launching of the first Sputnik. Two other books — *Peace and War: A Theory of International Relations* (1962) and *The Great Debate* (1963) — treat in greater detail certain problems touched on here.

I have asked myself why the American publisher proposed a new edition, thereby recognizing implicitly that the book retains a certain interest — a matter of which I was not sure. Perhaps the subtitle of the French edition suggests an answer: *armes atomiques et diplomatie planétaire*. What influence has been exercised on the course of international relations by the two major new elements of the post-war situation: the development of nuclear armaments and the extension of the diplomatic field to the entire planet? The question presents itself with as much force in 1967 as in 1956.

Of the three schools of thought that I distinguish —
the pessimistic school, which fears a nuclear holocaust,
the optimistic school which believes in peace through
fear, and the school of realists who coldly consider the
diplomacy of the atomic age to be modified by technology but not radically transformed — this third, to
which I belong, has up to now had the last word. The
maintenance of what is called "the balance of terror"
seemed to me in 1956 to be the most probable eventuality. In 1967, after eleven years of research in universities and institutes, after innumerable controversies
over the missile gap and over first and second strike
capabilities, it has been proclaimed by the American
Secretary for Defense that each of the two Great Powers
possesses today, and will possess tomorrow, a second
strike capability: in other words, the victim of a surprise attack would still retain means of reprisal sufficient
to inflict so-called unacceptable damage on the
aggressor.

During the 1961 electoral campaign President Kennedy feared the Soviet superiority in ballistic missiles;
in 1962 or 1963 Mr. McNamara stated that the United
States still possessed a first strike capability, that is to
say, the capacity to destroy a substantial fraction of
Soviet retaliatory forces; in 1967 he testified against the
installation of the anti-ballistic missile, convinced that
neither of the two Great Powers could any longer be
assured of a significant superiority in case of total war:
no matter who struck first, both of them would undergo
intolerable destruction.

From this fundamental position there follows the
series of questions formulated in this book, which do
not yet permit categorical answers.

1. If the armaments race does not promise either of
the two Great Powers a decisive advantage, why do

they not agree to end it? In the last eleven years, both the Russians and the Americans have multiplied their attempts. The Treaty of Moscow on the partial suspension of nuclear tests signifies a *voluntary agreement between enemies*. The anti-missile defenses that the Soviets have installed around Leningrad and Moscow, whose principle Secretary McNamara finally accepted in 1967, marks the limit of this agreement.

2. Of two possible agreements, one with the enemy, the other with its allies, the United States has chosen the first without much hesitation. An understandable choice, to be sure. A wise choice? The future will tell. The price of this choice is the weakening of Atlantic solidarity. The hostility of President Kennedy and his advisers to the French *force de frappe* contributed to the deterioration of relations between Paris and Washington, just as the 1959 denunciation of the Sino-Soviet treaty signed in 1957 contributed to the rupture between Moscow and Peking. Nuclear arms tend to bring enemies closer together and to separate allies, because the enemies discover their common interest in not fighting each other and in reserving to themselves the possession of nuclear weapons.

3. Optimists and pessimists, up to the present, have both been wrong, and for the same reason. Both underestimated the ingenuity, whether diabolical or reassuring, of man. Both failed to recognize the logic, not foreseen in advance but clearly evident after the fact, of the atomic universe. It is impossible to prevent every recourse to arms by threatening every enemy or aggressor with massive reprisals, a fact which dispels the illusion of a peaceful world through the fear of war. On the other hand, it is supremely improbable that the two Great Powers will abandon themselves to the folly of total war, as they have done twice in this century. Between non-violence and unlimited violence, the

powers now recognize innumerable intermediate positions.

4. In 1956 I presented these alternatives: *keep the peace by the threat of an ever more horrible war* or *find new distinctions between the modalities of war in order to limit its violence,* and I recommended the latter. The heads of state have not reasoned otherwise. To save humanity from thermonuclear war, they have saved war. Never in the course of the first two decades of the atomic age have the states possessing the supreme weapons engaged in armed conflict with each other. Twice, first in Korea, then in Vietnam, American divisions have fought on the Asiatic continent against troops, regular or irregular, of a Communist state. The U.S.–Soviet confrontation in the fall of 1962 over Soviet missiles in Cuba was reduced to an exchange of threats and messages.

The interest of this new edition probably centers in the contrast between the permanence of fundamental problems and the instability of local situations. I analysed these situations in 1956 less in-and-of themselves than in connection with ultimate questions: nuclear arms and the unity of the diplomatic field. That these questions should have remained the same while the situations in Europe, the Middle East, and Asia have changed seems to me to carry a lesson. The powers have discovered, at least for the time being, the secret of prolonging *diplomacy as usual* in an inchoate world. Neither peace through fear, nor peace through empire, nor peace through law. Neither a universal empire nor world federation. It is by drinking at the well of age-old wisdom that our Faustian civilization has resisted the fascination of the abyss. To limit violence by moderation, to renounce the pride of absolute victory, to tailor the use of force to the importance of the stakes — these precepts, as old as civilization itself, take on new meaning in a time when war puts in jeopardy not only the independence of nations, but the destiny of humanity.

RAYMOND ARON

Paris
October 1967

Preface

The following essay was written in August 1956 and published in April 1957 in a book entitled *Espoir et peur du siècle*—hope based on the possibility, thanks to economic progress, of a gradual enrichment of classes and nations, fear based on the threat of the annihilation of the human species by thermonuclear bombs. It seemed preferable to publish the essay on war separately in English, the rest of the book being too closely linked to problems peculiar to France.

In other times, a sociologist without specialist qualifications would have hesitated to deal with the problems of military strategy. He would at any rate have felt it necessary to apologize to his readers for doing so. It seems to me that such apologies are old-fashioned now; even Clemenceau's wisecrack about war being too serious an affair to be left to soldiers is now an understatement. Humanity has entered an unprecedented phase in which the great powers are, for the first time in history, preparing for a war they do not want to fight. How long can peace be preserved by the threat of a suicidal war? Is it possible to find a way out of the terror stalemate? No one is qualified to give a positive answer to such questions. And if no one can claim to be an expert, the sociologist is neither more nor less entitled than anyone else to indulge in these hazardous but necessary speculations.

ON WAR

Atomic Weapons and
Global Diplomacy

All military science becomes a matter of simple
prudence, its principal object being to keep an
unstable balance from shifting suddenly to our
disadvantage and the proto-war from changing
into total war.

CLAUSEWITZ

WHEN two atom bombs laid waste Hiroshima and
Nagasaki in August 1945, scientists, writers, and politicians proclaimed that humanity was entering a new
era, and each reverted to one of his favorite ideas.

The *optimists* saw in the diabolical weapon the
promise that this time "war was going to end war";
the nuclear explosive would accomplish what had been
vainly expected of gunpowder; peace would reign at
last, thanks to the progress of technology, not to a universal change of heart.

The *pessimists* heralded the approach of the apocalypse. The Faustian West, carried away by a satanic
impulse, would be punished for defying the gods and
refusing to recognize the limits of the human condition;
having divined the secrets of the atom, it possessed
the sovereign capacity to destroy both itself and others;
why should it suddenly find wisdom when for centuries
it had sought nothing but practical knowledge and
power?

The *realists*, rejecting both these extremes, left the future open. Between atomic peace and the annihilation of the species they perceived a middle way: no single weapon—however revolutionary—suffices to change human nature; political trends depend on men and societies as much as on weapons; if an atomic war is an absurd possibility for all the belligerents, it will not take place, though this does not mean that history will be exempt from the law of violence. . . .

The ten years which have elapsed since the thunderclaps of Hiroshima and Nagasaki have not enabled us to settle the argument. Today, just as ten years ago, we are equally free to imagine the final holocaust of civilization, the pacification of the world because of the impossibility of war ("There is no alternative to peace," as President Eisenhower has said), or else the continuation of history as a result of the limitation of conflicts.

The defenders of each of these arguments assail the proponents of the others with contempt. How can you possibly believe, cry the pessimists, that men who are incapable of outlawing atomic weapons will be capable of not using the bombs they so jealously cling to? If they are mad in peacetime, can you believe they will be sane when war breaks out?

Come now, reply the realists, if you consider humanity insane enough to launch an atomic war, how can you expect it to have the wisdom to come to an agreement on the terms of a total disarmament? Does it make sense to be afraid of the thermonuclear apocalypse and at the same time to hope for eternal peace or even for the return, by a concerted decision, to "pre-atomic innocence"? Contributors to the *Bulletin of Atomic Scientists* ridicule the "Utopian nostalgia" of limited wars, but since they do not believe in the permanence of a peace based on reciprocal terror, they ultimately revert to the "universal clamor for an end to history as a succession of wars."[1]

I belong, by temperament rather than conviction, to the realist school. The atomic weapon has not radically altered the trend of international politics. It has played a concealed part in the course of events; it has not caused the suicide of nations nor has it ensured peace and justice. . . . I do not therefore assume that the prophets of salvation or of catastrophe will be wrong tomorrow, but content myself with a lesson in method. The means of combat are *one* of the data of the political system, within states and between states. In the long run the action of military technique is perhaps decisive, but at any given moment it combines with other forces. The atom bomb, developed at a moment when two states were overwhelmingly more powerful than all the others, has reinforced the bipolar structure of the diplomatic field. On the other hand, once the bomb is at the disposal of every state, it will contribute to the dissolution of this structure.

Any analysis, whether of the recent past or the near future, must take into account simultaneously the consequences of the atomic innovation and the global situation. Not that the basic alternatives should be ignored. As the military revolution develops or accelerates, the two arguments which divide the commentators, from the humblest to the most exalted, from the journalist to the Nobel Prize-winning philosopher, take on a growing force. Does the thermonuclear bomb eliminate the danger of war by the fear which it inspires? Or must the atom and hydrogen bombs be abolished in order to avoid the horror of total war? At first glance, each of these two lines of reasoning appears convincing. Why should humanity be more peaceful tomorrow than it was yesterday, assuming that nuclear weapons have been effectively outlawed?

[1] E. Rabinovitch. January 1950. P. 32.

But if we stake the existence of humanity on the absence of war and lose our bet, we lose everything. It was reasonable to accept odds of ten to one on a traditional war three times a century; is it reasonable to accept odds of a hundred to one against a thermonuclear war once a century?

In other words, if we choose one of the two alternatives we reduce the probability of war, but immeasurably increase the havoc it would cause if it did break out. If we choose the other alternative, we increase the probability of a less devastating war. If one could estimate with any precision the probability factor and the extent of the destruction caused by each of the two types of war, the problem would allow of a theoretical solution. The fact is that we are incapable of going beyond the banal proposition that "thermonuclear war becomes improbable because of the terror it inspires."

Despite this uncertainty we know enough about the effects of the kind of thermonuclear bomb already available to choose between the two alternatives. In its issue of January 21, 1956, *The Economist* envisaged the explosion of a hydrogen bomb of ten megatons (equivalent to ten million tons of TNT) in the center of London:

"Everything within four miles of the centre of the fireball would be totally destroyed, much of it turned into dust and vapour and sucked up in the mushrooming cloud. The greater part of the County of London would be damaged beyond repair. The heat of the explosion would start a ring of fires that might extend for ten miles, right into the suburbs. People 16 miles away could be blistered by the heat and the buildings round them severely damaged by blast. Windows would be broken and tiles shaken in Kenley and Uxbridge, 24 miles from the centre of the explosion. The radio-active dust sucked up in the blast and the fireball would . . . float for 200 miles or more downwind far beyond sight or sound of the explosion, falling all the while and poisoning everything that it touched. Contamination from a bomb on Liverpool could almost reach the Thames estuary . . ."

This description, which is destined for the layman, may not be strictly scientific. The effects of nuclear explosions vary according to whether they occur in the air or at ground level. Nevertheless if one hydrogen bomb can cause such destruction as is described here —and we have no reason to doubt that it can—the number of H-bombs necessary to paralyze a nation like France or Great Britain can be counted on the fingers of both hands. The number would of course increase to a few dozen in the case of large countries such as the United States or the Soviet Union. With these considerations in mind, *if we had the choice*, we would prefer a war which was more probable but less devastating (all the more so because, according to the geneticists, a total thermonuclear war would endanger the survival of the species). But have we the choice?

The truth is that humanity—and this applies to statesmen as much as to ordinary citizens—has never had the choice. Attempts at disarmament in the past have always failed, but the attempt at atomic disarmament had even less chance of success because the nature of the weapons aroused additional obstacles to an agreement and even more to the supervision of such an agreement.

Optimists and pessimists are concerned with the future. Only the realists deal with the present—that is, with a world in which two states have the means of destroying one another and are therefore condemned to suicide or coexistence. In this present which must be measured in years, perhaps in decades, politics do not radically change; they do not exclude violence within nations or in the relations between states. Neither alliances nor revolutions nor traditional armies have disappeared. Frontiers are not unchangeable, transfers of sovereignty have not abated. More than ever, the diplomatic field is a jungle in which "cold-blooded monsters" are at grips with each other. More than ever, all possible means are resorted to—all except one, the use of which might well be fatal and which nevertheless profoundly influences the course of events, just as the British fleet used to assure the freedom of the seas, while anchored at its bases.

I. The Failure of
Atomic Disarmament

EFFORTS to limit, reduce, or abolish armaments have always been paralyzed by an internal contradiction. States are in essence sovereign. The right to independence in the taking of major decisions, those on which peace, war, or the status of citizens depend, has been asserted by cities, empires, and national states, by all collectivities which claimed to be autonomous, by all peoples who aspired to a political existence. The democratic city-states were no less jealous of their independence than the aristocratic ones, and the nations which in Europe assumed the heritage of the monarchies were no less jealous of their liberty than the kings had been of their glory. Sovereign states are automatically rivals. Not that all are by nature dedicated to indefinite expansion; insularity and self-sufficiency, the impulse to reduce relations with the outside world to a minimum, are no less *natural*, if rarer, than the appetite for endless conquest. At any given period certain states would have preferred tranquillity to adventure, the *status quo* to the risk of conflict. But states which refuse to submit to common laws cannot but regard one another with suspicion. How could they all be satisfied together? How accede to the reasonable demands of a dissatisfied state without arousing unreasonable claims? Experience shows that the ambition of states is more often sharpened than appeased by concessions.

Relations between sovereign states may be more or less bellicose; they are never *essentially* or *ultimately* peaceful. To eliminate the possibility of war is to deprive states of the right to be the ultimate judges of what the defense of their interests or their honor demands. Would it not be contradictory for states to agree to disarm if they reserved the right to take the law into their own hands?

After 1918, pacifists believed that the cause of war had been an armed peace. On the assumption that there are no genuine issues at stake, that conflicts arise from misunderstandings, that no state is prone to expansion, that war psychosis and war itself are created by the accumulation of arms on either side of a frontier, then disarmament by its very nature would ensure peace. By abolishing the instruments of warfare one would automatically abolish the will to fight. No one today would uphold so naïve a view. In an age like ours, states, classes, passions, interests clash in such confusion that war and not peace seems to be the natural order of things. In exceptional circumstances, when states subscribe to the same system of values or code of conduct, when national institutions are stabilized, when all the belligerents, even the victors, would have gained more from compromise than conflict, wars appear to be merely the effect of misunderstandings: there seems to be no other cause of war than the warlike passion itself, and people dream of extinguishing it by removing the instruments of glory.

If disarmament does not eliminate the cause of wars, what can be the point of it? There are two possible interpretations: either the effort to forbid the use of arms which humanity regards as particularly horrible, or the hope of states that by limiting the size of their armaments they can give evidence of their good intentions and by this very fact create an atmosphere of peace. The banning of poison gas on the one hand, and the Washington Naval Agreement of 1921 on the other, illustrate these two theoretical cases. The signatories reserved the right to fight, but they wanted to make their combats less cruel or less likely.

The attempts made in 1945-46 to prevent an atomic-arms race were regarded by American statesmen as radically original. In their eyes, the atom bomb represented a fundamental break in the course of history; within a few years it would provide mankind with the means of destroying itself. Thus the technological revolution would have to be met by a political revolution. From Washington's point of view the Baruch-Lilienthal plan represented such a revolution. It proposed the transference to an international agency of the ownership of atomic plants and raw materials. Internationalizing the development of atomic industry would prevent any clandestine use of nuclear energy for military ends.

There is little point in recalling in detail the objections officially raised by the Soviet representatives (the problem of the veto, the sequence and duration of the different phases, etc.). Perhaps the distinction, on which the plan relied, between the "enriched" uranium and the materials from which the manufacture of the bombs was possible had only a relative value. Peaceful uses and military uses are less easily separable than was believed ten years ago. What is significant here is the extent to which the failure of the attempt was logical and inevitable as long as people continued to think along traditional lines.

Whatever her regime, whether Communist or Czarist, Russia was bound to find herself one of the two great world powers after the defeat of Germany and she was bound to regard the United States as a rival. The incompatibility of the Russian and American ideologies reinforced an opposition that was implicit in the classic game of diplomacy. In agreeing not to acquire "know-how," even if the United States consented to destroy its stock of bombs at a later date, the Soviet Union (or the Russian Czarist Empire) would have had to resign itself to a permanent inferiority. Supposing a war broke out between the Big Two: the United States would have been capable of manufacturing bombs more rapidly than its enemy. From Moscow's point of view, the international agreement which would have prevented the atomic-arms race would have resulted in the stabilization of America's lead.[1] *An agreement on partial disarmament has no serious chance of being approved unless it gives neither side an advantage, in appearance or in reality.* In 1946, the Baruch-Lilienthal plan seemed to favor the United States, both in peacetime, because it would have withdrawn from the jurisdiction of national sovereignty the expansion of an industry vital for the prosperity of the world, and in wartime, because it would have left the United States in sole possession of the secret of manufacturing the terrifying weapon and almost bound to win the second race for it which would inevitably have started as soon as a new war was declared.

States which contemplated fighting each other could neither renounce a weapon which might perhaps be decisive nor enter into a form of industrial co-operation which was incompatible with the practices and the demands of sovereignty. International inspectors would have *freely* crossed frontiers, would have *freely* entered factories; the aircraft of the international control commission would have *freely* flown across the terri-

---

[1] Retrospectively, this line of reasoning appears to be false. In fact the United States would not have been able to manufacture a stockpile of atom bombs and would have had to develop conventional armaments in time of peace. In the long run the West would have found it more difficult than the Soviet Union to dispense with atomic weapons.

tories of the Soviet Union and the United States; British, Russian, American, and French scientists would have worked together for the progress of science and technology. Indeed, the revolution would have shaken the very foundations of the present order; in tampering with the concept of sovereignty, it would have removed the cornerstone of political organization. If nuclear energy, a source of power in war and of well-being in peace, had been immediately exploited by humanity and not jealously guarded by sovereign states, then indeed technology would have opened a new era in history. One may deplore, but not be astonished by, the fact that the rulers of the world should have wanted to keep for themselves what appeared from 1945 onward to be the supreme instrument of power and wealth.

Attempts to distribute blame are futile, even if the responsibilities of the two sides are not equal. Russian regimes, whether Czarist or Communist, have carried suspicion of foreigners and the passion for secrecy to lengths unheard of in the West. The leaders of the Soviet Union, by reason of their doctrine, regard themselves as in a permanent state of war with countries not converted to the gospel of Marx and Lenin. The men of the Politburo were more hostile to the implications of an international agency for the control of atomic energy than the men in the White House. The international inspectors would have discovered almost nothing in the United States that they could not have learned by reading the daily press or the technical journals. Many spies are arrested in the Soviet Union, but espionage is difficult there: the benefits of an international agreement would not have been equitably shared.

As a nation the United States has not been especially peaceable but it professes a peaceable philosophy. In 1945 the Americans could readily envisage a world

where secret diplomacy and power politics had disappeared. They would perhaps have been prepared to
face the ultimate consequences of the Baruch-Lilienthal plan, if their principal interlocutor had shown
them what they were. But this interlocutor–rival,
though not necessarily bellicose (in the sense of favoring a major war), adheres to a philosophy of war. The
oppressed class frees itself by fighting; the transition
from one regime to another cannot occur without violence; the rejection of violence leads to the betrayal
characterized by Social Democracy, to the illusory be-
lief that humanity will accede to socialism without
passing through the purgatory of revolution. The class
struggle, which does not necessarily entail the collision
of the two blocs, precludes trust and co-operation between capitalist and socialist countries. It precludes,
in other words, precisely what the plan for international control was aiming at.

The fact that the Big Two were not equally enthusi-
astic about the internationalization of atomic energy,
and the fact that their philosophies were incompatible
with one another—these data of world politics were not
indissolubly linked to the development of atomic weapons. It was a question of chance, of *hasard,* in Cour-
not's sense of the word. The sequence of events which
led up to the Hiroshima bomb, that which led to the
creation of the Soviet regime, and the one which led
to the domination of two peripheral powers are con-
nected with one another in many different ways, but
they did not spring from a common source. The progress of theoretical physics, the triumph of the Marxist
ideology in Russia, and the exhaustion of the European
states by the wars of the twentieth century—each of
these events obeys a certain logic. Technological civilization is responsible for the total character of modern
wars, for proletarian Messianism, and for the splitting

of the atom; but their conjunction itself was not pre-scribed in the book of fate.

Yet one cannot say that the element of chance (that is, the consequences of the conjunction) today appears considerable. Was the internationalization of atomic energy by agreement between a Communist state and the United States inconceivable? Very well: would it have been much more likely had it required the con-sent of half a dozen states of similar strength?

In 1949 President Truman announced to the Ameri-can people the explosion of an atom bomb in the Soviet Union. The United States had lost the monopoly of the terrifying weapon. In 1952 and 1953 both the United States and the Soviet Union exploded the first fission-fusion-fission bombs, commonly known as hydrogen or H-bombs. In 1955 and 1956 the first H-bombs were dropped from Russian and American airplanes. The progressive reduction of atomic inequality was to elim-inate one of the obstacles to disarmament. The progress of atomic armaments was to create others, still more difficult to overcome.

To revert to the formula which we outlined above: a disarmament agreement between sovereign states that do not exclude the possibility of war can only be reached on condition that it does not favor either of the "chief contracting parties." The disarmament nego-tiations which have been proceeding for years at the United Nations lack genuine seriousness, since the pro-posals of each side are manifestly contrary to the legit-imate interests of the other.

Between 1946 and 1952 the Soviet Union enjoyed a vast superiority in "traditional" weapons. In Europe the army of the Atlantic Alliance was incapable of halting an attack even from the Soviet divisions sta-tioned outside the frontiers of Russia. In Asia half the American army found the utmost difficulty in conquering the army of one of the satellites of the Soviet Union, North Korea, and failed to win a decisive victory against the Chinese volunteers. Only the atomic weapon ensured a balance of strength between the two sides. "The outlawing of weapons of mass destruction" was for obvious reasons a theme of Communist propaganda, which aimed to debar the United States from eventually using the bomb, and to spread the conviction that any nuclear explosion would mark the beginning of the holocaust. I do not know if Soviet propaganda changed the course of events. Perhaps the American strategists decided that no targets in Korea justified the expense of nuclear bombs, which were at that time costly and rare. Perhaps, too, a defenseless Europe served as a hostage: the cities of the Old World would have paid for the destruction of those of the Soviet Union. In any case, the propaganda for the "outlawing of nuclear weapons" was stopped or slowed down when in Moscow's eyes it became no longer necessary. Why bother to arouse indignation against weapons which they themselves possessed and which they intended to keep? There was no longer any need to collect millions of signatures for the Stockholm Peace Appeal in order to dismantle the bomb or enjoin the American leaders to prudence: the Soviet bombs would do the job.

The Western powers could not subscribe to the outlawing of the nuclear weapon as long as the Soviet Union enjoyed a vast superiority in traditional armaments. They demanded as a *quid pro quo* a reduction of these and at the same time a rigid control of the application of such agreements; but they demanded these things without either the hope or the desire to obtain them. They knew that the Soviet Union would not tolerate the free circulation of international inspectors, either on land or in the air, and they could not conceive of any effective control without such freedom of movement. Moreover, if the Soviet Union had agreed to reduce its conventional armed forces, the West would not sincerely have renounced the atomic weapon, *which it could not dispense with in the event of war.* An agreement on the outlawing of weapons of mass destruction could not have been concluded in good faith, since it was bound to put one of the two sides in a state of irremediable inferiority.

The present reversal of the positions taken up by the different parties in the pseudo-negotiations on disarmament reveals better than any long speeches the intentions of the orators and the meaning of their words. The Soviet Union, while maintaining its ritual demand for the outlawing of the atomic weapon, insists on the limitation of conventional armaments. The Western powers, without opposing such a limitation, insist on the impossibility of reducing conventional weapons except in conjunction with atomic disarmament. Yesterday the West was unwilling to give up the nuclear weapon except in circumstances impossible of realization. Today the Soviets are no longer interested in a disarmament which would limit their power as much as that of their enemies.

It will be objected that logically the leaders of the two great powers have no further interest in keeping weapons which they cannot use without committing a sort of mutual suicide. This is to forget that the Big Two partly owe their supremacy over their allies and over the neutrals to these very weapons. Moreover, both the United States and the Soviet Union, having become the first atomic powers, thanks to the wealth of their resources, can less and less afford to dispense with this new acquisition.

The impossibility of disarmament springs first of all from the irreversible facts created by developments during the ten years since Hiroshima. In 1946 the question was how to avoid the clandestine manufacture of atom bombs. Today, each camp possesses a stockpile of bombs sufficient to devastate the other's territory: the question now is, or ought to be, how to guarantee the destruction of the existing stockpiles. *And to this question there is at present no answer.* Neither of the two great powers will destroy its own for fear of putting itself at the mercy of its rival should the latter break its pledge. In the foreseeable future, two states at least will possess the means to lay waste every city on the globe.

The evolution of military technique is also irreversible. The number of vehicles required to transport nuclear explosives is in inverse proportion to the power of those explosives. The American aviation strength is increasingly adapted to the nuclear weapon; it would not be great enough should there be any question of reverting to TNT. If, tomorrow, American divisions are organized and trained on the basis of tactical atomic weapons, no chief of state, unless he wishes to disarm his country, will be able to go back on these decisions taken long in advance. The weapons used in 1918 or in 1945 differed radically from the weapons of 1914 or of 1939, but the latter could not differ from the weapons manufactured in peacetime. If the Atlantic army is equipped entirely with atomic weapons, a European war will inevitably be an atomic war. Perhaps the decisions which in the future will appear most fateful have been taken in an atmosphere of general indifference during years of relative calm.

What basis can there be today for genuine negotiations on disarmament? The three possible objectives, it seems to me, are the stabilization or the reduction of conventional weapons, the suspension or the limitation of the nuclear-arms race, and the blackballing from the atomic club of powers which are not already members.

The first of these should arouse no very strong feelings. Whether the negotiations succeed or, as is more probable, fail—with or without an international agreement—the great powers will reduce the number of their divisions as they invest more heavily in atomic weapons. The demobilization, announced with a great flourish of trumpets, of several hundred thousand Russian soldiers is probably not so much a propaganda measure as the result of a rational calculation, military and economic. Why bother to maintain on a wartime basis divisions which could not be of use except in the case of a general war and whose very number would compel the enemy to resort to weapons of mass destruction?

This partial demobilization is all the more sensible in that it does not endanger Soviet superiority. The bloc of Communist states, from East Germany to North Vietnam, possesses regular armies[2] which, at virtually every point of the periphery would be capable of crossing frontiers and decisively defeating the troops with whom they came in contact. The only exception is Korea, where, it appears, the South is capable of standing up to the North. Everywhere else, the Communist state is militarily stronger than its non-Communist neighbor. The Chinese army is without a rival in Asia, the Russian army without a rival in Europe.

Would it have been otherwise if the United States had not created, as a result of their monopoly and their subsequent superiority in atomic armaments, an atmosphere of security through terror? This is debatable. On paper the West possesses fewer men (if one counts the Chinese masses) but more coal, steel, and oil.

Statistically speaking, Western Europe, with the aid

[2] Provided the armies of the satellites obey their leaders' orders. After the events in Poland and Hungary it is doubtful whether this condition applies in Europe. The armies of the satellite states are not an advantage but a handicap to the Soviet Union.

of the United States, would not find it difficult to defend itself. But totalitarian regimes impose on their people sacrifices which the democracies are unwilling to accept. Even in the age of technology, the traditional conflict between rich nations and poor still applies. In the past the rich nations owed their safety to the quality of their organization or their technology; they counterbalanced primitive violence with the resources of civilization. The peoples of the West, who are rich in relation to the Russian or Chinese masses, owe their provisional safety to the atomic weapon, which is to conventional weapons what the discipline of the Roman legion was to the fury of the Goths. (But the Soviets also know the secrets of civilization.)

Granted the superiority in conventional weapons of the Soviet camp, an agreement on the maximum number of troops allowed to each of the principal countries is conceivable. Owing to differences in organization and living standards, the Soviet Union, with the same number of men, will be able to put more divisions into the field than other countries. In time of war it will be easy for both sides to mobilize millions of men, assuming that nuclear or thermonuclear bombs leave the traditional armies something to conquer or defend.

Such an agreement on the basis of armed strength would not raise insurmountable difficulties but neither would it afford major advantages compared with the present situation. As an expression of good will and peaceful intentions, it would be an auspicious event. Nevertheless, it remains improbable, for three reasons. Statesmen are conscious of the fact that an agreement on numbers of divisions or guns in the age of the thermonuclear bomb would be comparable to an agreement on bows and arrows, lances, and spears in the age of the first firearms. The limitation of divisions which the West clamored for in vain when it enjoyed an atomic monopoly no longer interests anyone now that it is of so much less account. However unimportant, such a limitation is possible in the eyes of the West only if it is combined with a system of inspection and control. The system organized by the armistice of Korea or Indochina has failed. A less imperfect system still remains unacceptable to the Soviet leaders, obsessed by fear of espionage and a passion for secrecy. Finally, neither American nor Russian leaders are vitally interested in such an agreement. The Soviets prefer a breakdown of negotiations to strict control: the Americans prefer a breakdown of negotiations to imperfect control. Soon the armies of the other countries will automatically fall below the level which the diplomats have in mind for them.

Much more significant would be an agreement on a total or partial suspension of the atomic-arms race. But it must first be pointed out that such an agreement is improbable because it would at the same time entail the suspension of scientific research.

For the moment, two proposals are advanced by those who claim to be the interpreters of public opinion: the suspension of thermonuclear tests and the suspension of rocket development. The first proposal has been taken up by some politicians and it has played a role in presidential campaigns in the United States. British newspapers are always ready to support the idea that the two big powers should undertake voluntarily to suspend thermonuclear tests or at least to limit the number and the nature of such tests.

It is not easy for the layman to determine the extent to which technical means could ensure the observance of such a pledge. Let us assume that an international bureau installed in neutral territory is in a position to detect any thermonuclear explosion wherever it occurs. Let us assume that in this particular case the difficulties of inspection and control do not arise. Agreement remains nonetheless improbable for obvious reasons which it would be foolish to ignore on the pretext of saving humanity from the dangers which threaten it.

To be acceptable to the two great powers, the suspension of thermonuclear explosions would have to occur at a moment of approximate parity. Neither of them will tolerate a permanent position of inferiority. Does such parity exist today? Possibly, but neither side can be sure. The men responsible for American defense emphatically reject a measure which may perhaps be reasonable but which certainly goes against the grain of our scientific civilization. Faustian man will not voluntarily halt on the road to knowledge, even if it is also the road to catastrophe. Great Britain, which has also joined in the arms race, would postpone agreement until the day when she in her turn has mastered the secret. The experiments do not all tend to increase the power of the thermonuclear weapon. The same development which reduced the Hiroshima bomb to the dimensions of a shell can occur in the case of the thermonuclear bomb. As long as the use of the latter is not precluded, it is difficult to prohibit experiments and tests which would make it usable under different forms. Finally, do not these bomb tests offer lessons which could be applied to the peaceful uses of atomic energy? Having learned to control nuclear fission, why despair of learning to control nuclear fusion?

The second, and even more important, proposal concerns the researches in connection with intercontinental rockets. The thermonuclear bomb, whose explosive power can be counted in millions of tons of TNT instead of thousands as in the case of the Hiroshima bomb, followed a mere half-dozen years after the revolution that put a tragic stop to the forty years of war ushered in by the revolver shots which killed Archduke Ferdinand of Austria. A third military revolution is afoot, unknown to the public, under the mysterious initials IRBM (intermediate range ballistic missile) and ICBM (intercontinental ballistic missile).

Short-range rockets, earth-to-air, air-to-air and air-to-earth, are already available. Within a few years, according to the experts, the IRBM, with a range of several hundred miles, will be in operation and capable of being launched with reasonable accuracy. And, it appears, in only a few years more, Russian rockets with thermonuclear warheads will be able to strike at any city in the United States, and American rockets at any city in the Soviet Union. The civil and military experts who, in an atmosphere of general indifference, call for the prohibition of tests on intercontinental rockets, put forward a striking argument, comparable to the one advanced ten years ago by the American physicists and which events have confirmed: *tomorrow will be too late.* It was possible to control the manufacture of atom bombs; it is not possible to supervise the destruction of existing stockpiles. It is possible to control the airdromes from which the strategic air forces would take off; it will not be possible to supervise the rocket-launching sites. There is still a chance of avoiding the perfecting of intercontinental missiles; once this has happened there will be no going back. No one will know how to eliminate the rockets, just as no one knows how to eliminate the existing stockpiles of nuclear and thermonuclear weapons.

When that moment comes, the double revolution of fire power and movement will have finally reached its goal. A weapon with a fire power capable of devastating an entire city will be able to reach any point on the earth within a few minutes. The distance between the combatants, if one can so describe the man who presses the button and the man whose body is disintegrated by the explosion, will reach up to thousands of miles. It is ironic to think that only half a century separates the combination of fire power and

movement in the first tank and the same combination
in the intercontinental rocket with a thermonuclear
warhead.

The reasons which make the prohibition of thermonuclear tests unlikely make the prohibition of long-
distance rocket tests even more unlikely. The scientific
importance of these tests is obvious. The difficulties of
control are far greater (it would be necessary to set up
more and more radar stations all over the globe). The
banning of *all* rockets would affect a great number of
states. The banning of intercontinental rockets alone
would demand a rigid discrimination between short-
range and long-range rockets. Finally, the scientists of
each of the two great powers are so afraid of being
overtaken by their rivals and have such hunger for
total knowledge, that the choice of power in preference
to wisdom seems irresistible.

Only one incentive could halt this all-out arms race:
the wish to keep others from entering it. The suspension of nuclear tests would affect Great Britain and
the European countries more than the United States
or the Soviet Union. Perhaps the latter two will recognize that it is in their joint interest to keep to themselves alone the weapons of mass destruction and the
new missiles, faster than jet airplanes and free from
the limitations of human nature. But the time has not
yet arrived when they will rest on their laurels as the
sole members of the atomic club instead of continuing
to increase their fire power and speed of movement.
When the intercontinental rocket with a thermonuclear
warhead is available, how many states will belong to
the atomic club? Will the Big Two then be more
conscious of their solidarity than their rivalry? After
all, Athens and Sparta, had they been reasonable,
ought to have shared the empire between them instead
of exhausting themselves in search of an unattainable
triumph.

Disarmament has proved impossible for ten years because — and remains impossible as long as — states are "cold-blooded monsters" whose law is always to suspect, often to fight, and sometimes to destroy each other. Science helps men to kill one another by mass production; it does not teach them wisdom.

II. The Failure of
Traditional Rearmament

THE ten years which have elapsed since the end of
the Second World War have been rich in events un-
folding on two planes: on the politico-diplomatic level
the Sovietization of Eastern Europe, the civil war in
Greece, the secession of Yugoslavia, the Berlin blockade, the Communist victory in China, and the Korean
and Indochinese wars; on the technological and military level, the Anglo-American demobilization in 1946,
the explosion of the first Russian atom bomb in 1949,
the Western rearmament of 1950–53, and the manufacture of thermonuclear bombs. Can we discern, looking back, a relationship between diplomatic events and
military events?

One fact is immediately apparent. It was during the
years 1945–49, when the United States enjoyed an
atomic monopoly, that the Soviet Union won its greatest successes (the consolidation of the Communist
regimes in Eastern Europe, the conquest of power by
the Chinese Communist party). It was also during
these years that Moscow's diplomacy was most aggressive—in Czechoslovakia, in Berlin, at international con-
ferences, and in its propaganda. This aggressiveness
has sometimes been explained by the sense of weakness
Stalin and his henchmen must have felt, whereas ten
years later, sure of its strength, Russia presents a re-
laxed demeanor to the world. This interpretation,

which can neither be proved nor disproved, does not seem convincing to me: when Stalin was really frightened, face to face with Hitler, he behaved quite otherwise. The simpler and more probable explanation is that he had been frightened of Hitlerite Germany but was never frightened of Truman's America. And in both cases he was not far wrong. The United States, as far as one can judge, did not immediately accelerate the production of atom bombs. During the first postwar years, with their atomic monopoly, the Americans had the means of preventing the Soviet Union from launching an open attack; they did not have the means, traditional or otherwise, to enable them to impose their will.

The very enormity of the atomic weapon prevented the United States from using it as a diplomatic instrument, whatever the stockpiles available. Soviet propaganda would not have had the success it did, had it not coincided with a vague but powerful feeling among millions of people. A local conflict, or one where the issues were of minor importance, was not amenable to the bomb. It was not Communist Russia, it was the instinct of humanity which, on the morrow of Hiroshima and Nagasaki, invented the notion of a correlation between the size of a war and that of the weapons employed. Neither the victories of Mao Tse-tung, nor Markos's guerilla campaign, nor the Prague *coup d'état*, nor the Berlin blockade, nor even the invasion of Korea by Communist troops, justified atomic retaliation. The traditional balance between continental power and maritime power was revived at the beginning of the atomic age, though in a novel form: the capacity of the United States to devastate Russian cities against the capacity of the Soviet Union to occupy Western Europe. The horror inspired by the atomic weapon paralyzed the United States as much as or more than the Soviet divisions massed on the borders of a Europe incapable of defending itself.

One can, of course, speculate on what would have happened if the United States had sent an armed convoy to break the Berlin blockade, or had delivered an atomic ultimatum demanding the blockade's cessation. One is inclined, after the event, toward the opinion that Moscow would have given way. But both question and answer have equally little meaning. The American system precludes diplomacy of this sort, which moreover would have demanded other arms besides atom bombs alone. In any case, as a result of the balance between Soviet superiority in conventional weapons and the atomic superiority of the United States, because of America's democratic institutions, or simply because of an irresistible demand of the human conscience, it was assumed that the new weapon would be used only in exceptional circumstances. For the time being, the bomb guaranteed the invulnerability of the frontier drawn by the diplomats during the war to divide Germany into zones of occupation. It prevented invasion and a major war; it also prevented the solution of local problems.

It was not the explosion of the first atom bomb in Russia but the North Korean aggression which opened a second phase in the military history of the Cold War. Between the major war which would be waged with atom bombs, and the Cold War which forbade the use of regular armies, came a "hot local war." Once again, the war that occurred was not the war that had been prepared for. Events obliged statesmen and soldiers to reconsider the strategy of the atomic age. No one, on June 25, 1950, proposed that the crossing of the 38th parallel should be answered by an ultimatum to Moscow, no one proposed to retaliate by dropping atom bombs on Pyongyang, Peking, or Moscow. In fact, the choice was between nonintervention and a local campaign, and the second alternative was resolutely chosen. This choice was maintained to the end in spite of early reverses, in spite of the intervention of Chinese divisions.

The Korean War ended with an approximate return to the *status quo ante*. The new line of demarcation varied little from the 38th parallel. If the Americans, after having landed at Inchon and destroyed the North Korean army, had voluntarily halted at the old demarcation line they would have been able to claim that they were the victors and been acknowledged as such by chancelleries and men-in-the-street alike all over the world. But they had pushed on to the Yalu in order to re-establish the unity of Korea by force. They had failed. Certainly the Koreans had failed in their first offensive and the Chinese in their turn had failed when they attempted to fling the Eighth Army into the sea. But the United States is the strongest power in the world. Morally, America's non-victory was a defeat, as the Chinese non-defeat was a victory. Politically, this peace without victory in a limited war marked a turning point in the history of the twentieth century. In thirty years, from 1914 to 1944, humanity had passed from horses to internal-combustion engines, from rifles to atom bombs. In 1918 the Second Reich had laid down its arms but had not ceased to exist as a state. In 1944 the war had been brought to an end only by the junction of the Anglo-American and Russian armies in the center of Germany, the total destruction of the army of the Third Reich, and the temporary disappearance of the German state itself. To what orgies of violence would a third world war lead? In Korea, the two great powers made it abundantly clear that, for the time being at least, they did not want to wage a third world war.

The Korean War remained a limited war by a decision which was never officially confirmed but which determined the conduct of operations by both sides. The limitation concerned the number of belligerents, the theater of operations, the weapons employed, and the aims of the combatants.

In both world wars, each side endeavored to recruit allies and contributed to the extension of the struggle. Just as in the Peloponnesian War, according to Thucydides, the Persian Empire was finally involved in the inexpiable rivalry of Athens and Sparta, so in 1914–18 the soldiers of India and Africa came to fight each other on the Western Front. The Europeans, losing their sense of unity in the heat of battle, called on non-Europeans to help to settle a conflict which was to determine the hegemony over their continent, just as the Greeks had solicited and obtained the support of the barbarians against their fellow Greeks. It would have been easy to denounce the Soviet Union for aiding North Korea and China, or the use of Japanese territory as a base for the United Nations armies. Carrying the refusal to call a spade a spade as far as they had earlier carried the mobilization of the neutrals, the United States abstained from treating China as an enemy.

This desire to restrict the scope of the conflict expressed itself, as it were, symbolically, in the geographical limitation of hostilities. American aircraft did not bomb the Manchurian airports: the Manchurian sanctuary was respected to the end, as was the Japanese sanctuary. Not without some hesitation, the American leaders allowed themselves to be convinced that the non-generalization of the conflict (on which there was no divergence of opinion either among the Western powers or among Americans) demanded that the operations be restricted to Korean territory. The peninsula represented a battlefield within which the Sino-Korean and Americo-Korean armies measured their strength as though in the lists at a medieval tourney.

The non-use of atomic weapons followed logically from this double limitation of the number of belligerents and of the theater of operations. Perhaps the atomic weapons which the American forces had at their disposal at the time did not meet the requirements of the campaign: no town in North Korea (in the opinion of the American aviation experts) was worth an atom bomb. Moreover, the memory of Hiroshima and Nagasaki continues to haunt the relations between Americans (and perhaps Europeans) and Asians. If for a second time a "yellow" people had been the victims of the diabolical weapon, the whole of Asia would have seen in it a proof of "white" racism. Finally, perhaps the Western statesmen vaguely thought that atomic weapons necessarily involved total war, a false notion by which they expressed the truth that every war does not call for the use of every weapon.

After this triple limitation, a last and decisive one became inevitable: a limitation of war aims. Obviously China could not be forced into unconditional surrender if the fighting was restricted to the Korean battlefield. A negotiated peace was the inevitable result of the restrictions which the belligerents had imposed on themselves.

This strategy was adopted only after long debate, and today one is tempted to conclude that neither MacArthur's supporters nor his adversaries were entirely in the right. MacArthur's famous slogan, "There is no substitute for victory," is either a truism or a dangerous error, according to the meaning one gives it. If it means that nothing can replace military victory, that is to say the destruction of the enemy's armed forces, it merely revives the conception unfortunately adopted by Roosevelt during the Second World War. The destruction of the enemy army obviously enables the victor to dictate the terms of the peace treaty, but a dictated peace is not always preferable to a negotiated peace. Politics must decide.[1]

Or the phrase simply means that the aim of any war is to create a situation more favorable than that which existed before hostilities began. Victory consists in obtaining, through war, either territory or security, either the weakening of an enemy or the strengthening of an ally. In that case, there is indeed no alternative to victory except defeat, but the proposition is simply a tautology.

Of these two interpretations, the first is the one which probably comes nearer to MacArthur's ideas and intentions, certainly nearer to those of his supporters. But MacArthur's opponents were inclined to err in the opposite direction by confusing the renunciation of total victory with the renunciation of any victory at all; by posing the single option "total war or a draw." The return to the *status quo ante* was the inevitable consequence not of the limitation of the conflict but of the refusal to engage the forces necessary to a partial and local victory.

The controversy about the Manchurian airfields had less military significance than was suggested by the politicians and commentators. The Russian MIG fighters did not play a serious part on the battlefield. Even if the American bombs had destroyed them on the ground nothing would have been changed at the 38th parallel. Nor did the MIGs prevent the bombing of the Sino-Korean communication lines. On the other hand, if, in September 1950, after the Inchon landing and the capture of Pyongyang, the Eighth Army had established itself across the "waist" of the peninsula, the Chinese armies would have been unable to get from the Yalu to the front. In the same way, if, in the spring of 1951, the Eighth Army had not been halted

[1] In this sense Clausewitz's dictum, "War is the continuation of politics by other means," has no militaristic significance at all.

by the armistice negotiations, it would probably have been able to push back the enemy troops beyond Pyongyang. It would also have been able to win victories in 1952 and 1953 if it had been reinforced by two or three divisions.

With a more skillful conduct of the campaign or an increased military effort the United States would have been able to obtain more favorable armistice terms. (The armistices in Kashmir, Palestine, and Korea are limited to stabilizing the fighting lines.)

The Korean War prompted the civil and military leaders of the West to ask themselves some basic questions: What sort of war, or rather what sorts of wars, should we now prepare for? What are the ends and the means of our strategy?

Nothing was more striking in this connection than the uncertainty of the generals about the meaning of the Korean campaign. Both General Bradley, the head of the Joint Chiefs of Staff in Washington, and the German General Guderian, discussing the strictly military concepts of an enemy and a theater, saw in the Korean campaign a foolish dispersal of forces, a war "in the wrong place at the wrong time against the wrong enemy." But if the two sides were determined not to wage a total war, the Korean campaign was the right war in a relatively favorable place at an opportune time (since the United States still enjoyed atomic superiority which guaranteed the limitation of the conflict). On the outcome of the Korean campaign depended, in part, the political evolution of Asia, that is to say, one of the major issues of the Cold War.

The same uncertainty about the meaning of these events is discernible in the European rearmament program precipitately decided upon in the autumn of 1950. The crossing of the 38th parallel by the North Korean armies did not foreshadow the crossing of the European demarcation line by the Soviet divisions. In fact, one might have drawn from the Korean episode precisely the opposite lesson: since the Soviets were going out of their way, in spite of hostilities in Asia, to reduce the risks of a generalized conflict, there was no reason to fear an aggression in Europe which would infallibly have provoked a world war. Nevertheless, the rearmament of Europe in the autumn of 1950 was based on three reasonable arguments. As long as their peoples had no fear of war, the Western statesmen could leave Europe open to invasion, secure in the conviction that the atomic weapon would suffice to prevent the advance of the Red divisions toward the Atlantic. From the moment when, rightly or wrongly, events awoke the fear of a general war, when Communist propaganda proclaimed that "Bonn would soon meet the same fate as Seoul," the building up or strengthening of the army defending Western Europe became imperative if only for psychological reasons.

Moreover, the Korean experience proved the possibility of a non-atomic war in the atomic age. Within a few years the Soviet Union would have caught up with the West in the field of nuclear weapons: Who would threaten to destroy the enemy's cities if he knew that his own were open to reprisals? A progressive equalization of traditional forces seemed to be the answer to the coming phase of atomic parity.

Finally, a Europe with no other defense but the atom bomb would serve, so to speak, as a hostage to the Soviet Union. Western diplomacy was hamstrung, its politico-psychological action paralyzed, by the disproportion between the number of divisions stationed on each side of the Iron Curtain.

These reasons, good or bad, but in any case understandable, possibly played a smaller part in the decision to rearm than the contagious panic provoked by the Korean battles. The autumn of 1950 saw the beginning of a second phase in the military policy of the

Atlantic Alliance. It was decided to reinforce the atomic weapon with a certain number of "traditional divisions." The question was, how many?

To decide this, two criteria seem to have been invoked successively or perhaps simultaneously. The *ideal* number would have been enough to enable the NATO armies to halt a full-scale attack by the divisions of the Soviet bloc without recourse to the atomic weapon. A smaller number would enable them to stop an attack by the Soviet divisions stationed outside the frontiers of Russia. A still smaller number would suffice to prevent raids and surprise attacks and *faits accomplis* which could not be altered except by a total war. In the first case, a general non-atomic war was envisaged. In the second, the enemy was forced to reveal his preparations in advance. In the third, the conventional divisions would have no other function than that of a "fire alarm."

The rearmament of Western Europe began with the first conception, slipped into the second, and has wound up today at the third. This development was probably inevitable, but it was precipitated by the mistakes committed in the process of traditional rearmament.

Although the public is little aware of it, the European rearmament has been effected under almost unbelievable conditions. It has set a record in cost and inefficiency; it would be difficult to imagine how more money could be spent for fewer weapons and weapons of more doubtful worth. The American division chosen as the standard for the European divisions represented an "improved version" of the American division of 1944, with heavier tanks, more vehicles, and increased fire power, but also even more complex services and a smaller number of front-line troops in relation to the size of the division.

Even in the United States, with a population of more

than 160 millions and a gross national income of 350,-
000 billion dollars, such a system can produce only a
small number of divisions (about twenty-five in the
1952 program). When adopted by the European nations, it was responsible for the startling contrast between comparable forces on each side of the Iron Curtain, and an enormous inequality in heavy units. True,
divisions are not always the same, and American divisions (or Atlantic divisions) are on paper equivalent
to more than one division of the Soviet type. But even
if one Atlantic division is equivalent to one and a half
Soviet divisions, the gap between the traditional forces
of the two sides remains considerable.

The waste of man power has been accompanied
by a waste of money. Modern weapons—tanks, armored cars, aircraft, antiaircraft artillery—are expensive everywhere. And the perpetual search for perfection makes them more expensive in the Western
camp than in the other. In any case the solution
adopted was obviously not the right one. If a European
country is incapable of maintaining more than a dozen
American-type divisions it must adopt another standard. After all, the Swiss peasants would never have
been able to equip as many cavalrymen as the Bur-
gundians, but they nevertheless remained undefeated.

Apart from their expense, the efficiency of the improved American-type divisions of 1944 is debatable.
With their three thousand vehicles, their daily needs
of one thousand tons of gasoline, munitions, and food,
are they capable of operating without being protected
against the enemy air forces? In 1944–45 the Anglo-
American air forces enjoyed a total mastery of the
skies. It is difficult to imagine that the same situation
will repeat itself.

The West's inferiority in traditional weapons, which
is commonly ascribed to the difference in political regimes and standards of living (these explanations are

not entirely false), is also attributable to the error of taking as a prototype for heavy units the mechanical monsters of 1944–45, the Europeans here following the example of the Americans without either their wealth or their industrial potential. This error is all the more surprising in that it coincides, if we are to believe the military experts, with striking advances in the development of light defensive weapons. Fifty-ton tanks costing nearly $200,000 were manufactured which can be destroyed by hollow-charge shells fired by an individual soldier. Heavy divisions were built up which the evolution toward the atomic weapon and toward individual weapons makes doubly vulnerable.

When the goal of one hundred divisions was recognized as unattainable without a mobilization of national economies impossible in peacetime, when the target figure was brought down to sixty and finally even lower, the planners of SHAPE, who had been entrusted with the task of repelling an eventual attack from the Soviet army, had to seek another solution. Technological progress seemed the obvious answer. The atomic weapon no longer boiled down to the "big bomb" of Hiroshima and Nagasaki which had failed to find worthy targets in Korea. Just as the Hiroshima bomb is absurdly small compared to the H-bombs of today or tomorrow, it is gigantic compared with atomic shells.

At the time of the Korean War there had been a cut-and-dried distinction between a local war waged with traditional weapons and a general war waged with atomic weapons. Henceforth the alternatives envisaged were local wars waged with tactical atomic weapons or a general war in which tactical atomic weapons would be used in the land battles while the strategic air forces, far behind the front lines, would strike at the heart of enemy territory.

But at once a new debate began, a debate that was

more political than military. European rearmament had first been conceived with a view to a non-atomic war, or at least a non-atomic defense of the Continent. What would be the point of an Atlantic army equipped with atomic artillery? Should it complement or preclude strategic bombing? In the event of the destruction of cities in belligerent countries by H-bombs, was a battle between organized mass armies still conceivable? If one imagined land warfare with tactical atomic weapons as a substitute for strategic bombing, wasn't one the victim of an illusion? The belligerents would not stop halfway. The atomic shells would first of all aim at concentrations of troops and airports, but the range of destruction and the lack of precision would be such that the nearby cities would be affected. And why should the cities near the armies be the only ones privileged to serve as targets? Irresistibly, the belligerents would enlarge the theater of aerial operations. From then on, where would the line be drawn between the tactical and the strategic, between atomic artillery and the A- and H-bombs?

The drift toward total war seems to such an extent irresistible that the planners have taken it for granted from the start. Six years after the beginning of the rearmament, the experts of SHAPE are resigned to a situation which the statesmen recognized in 1950 and out of which they hoped to find a way: *for Europe, there is no middle way between peace and annihilation.* On the Continent, the West defends itself by awakening the fear of total disaster. The only strategy is the strategy of what the Anglo-Saxons call the "deterrent." For the first time in history men are preparing for a type of war they do not wish to fight and refusing to prepare for another, as though they ran the risk of preserving war by providing it, even hypothetically, with another aspect than that of mutual annihilation. Who would set fire to his neighbor's house if he was sure of starting a conflagration from which he himself would not escape?

It is doubtless inaccurate to regard the outcome of the military policy begun in 1950 as indistinguishable from the original situation. In 1950 the West had to adapt itself to the loss of its atomic monopoly. In 1956 atomic parity is admitted, at least hypothetically. In 1950 conventional divisions were combined with atom bombs. In 1956 the bombs of the strategic air forces are H-bombs, whose power must be reckoned no longer in kilotons but in megatons. Refusing to believe possible or desirable a war in which the use of atomic artillery would not lead to the use of thermonuclear weapons, the Western strategists appear to have no alternative plans between which to choose at the critical moment. The land armies no longer have the function, even hypothetically, of waging a war in which the thermonuclear horror would not be unleashed; their sole function is to create the *casus belli atomici.* They must be numerous enough and well enough equipped to prevent a surprise attack and to fight a battle the size of which would justify a recourse to the ultimate means. Secondarily, if the struggle lasted more than a few days (though the experts do not know precisely what the time divisions of the atomic age should be), the armies would protect what remained of the national territory against what survived of the enemy troops.

We have lived through a revolution in both senses of the word—a military innovation, in that the Hiroshima bomb has given birth to atomic shells and thermonuclear bombs, but an innovation which has restored, in an entirely different form, the initial problem: the West has failed to find a substitute for total war other than peace itself.

A symbol of this failure is the Pentagon's proposal to cut the Army and the Navy in order to concentrate on building up the Air Force. Once again, the press and common sense alike protest against this military doctrine which threatens, on each occasion, to force the West into a choice between capitulation or suicide. Once more the peoples of the West, rulers and public alike, are alarmed at a reduction in traditional forces, even though these are reputed to be anachronistic and useless.

Men persist in attaching value to the number of soldiers under arms, although the experts continue to harp on the futility of these evidences of a bygone age. Men refuse to follow the experts' logic to its ultimate conclusion. There is no alternative to peace, reiterates President Eisenhower, who agrees with his advisers that a war between the great powers would be a thermonuclear war. But the chorus of the backward or the wise echoes in reply: should we not maintain a substitute for thermonuclear war?

So runs the dialogue in which each speaker, according to the day and the mood, feels ready to play either part, so strongly is each opposed to the other, so weak within himself.

III. Unity and Plurality
of the Diplomatic Field

THE international situation at the end of the Second World War was characterized by four main features: the supremacy of Russia and the United States; the military presence of these two states at every point of the globe; their mutual ideological antagonism; and the development of weapons of mass destruction. None of these features, except the last, was unprecedented. But their conjunction was new, and the novelty can be shown in several different ways: the atomic weapon was introduced at a time when all the nations of the world constituted a single system dominated by two giants, each of which seemed pledged by its very nature to seek the destruction of the other.[1] When the collapse of European states and empires created a vacuum in Europe and Asia, two states faced each other, the one irresistible on land, the other, thanks to the atomic weapon, in the air, each convinced that it alone could show humanity the road to freedom.

Let us take as a point of departure the least original situation: the bipolar structure which historical memories—Athens and Sparta, Rome and Carthage, Caesar

[1] The United States is pledged to seek the death of Communism only to the extent that the latter refuses to recognize and cannot recognize, according to its doctrine, the right of capitalism to exist.

and Antony—charge with tragic overtones. When two states outclass all others, their relations are likely to take one of four different forms. They can rule together over the civilization to which they both belong; they can draw a dividing line between the zones which constitute their respective empires; they can engage in a struggle to the death; or they can coexist as enemies. These four possibilities might be boiled down to two: complete or partial agreement, total or limited conflict.

There is another possible formula, less logical but historically more accurate: complete agreement or a struggle to the death being ruled out, the reality would consist of a combination between the partition of the world into zones of influence and competition for frontiers and the allegiance of neutrals. Cold war and peaceful coexistence are merely two variations of this same compound of tacit understanding and open rivalry. In one case, the leaders put the accent on rivalry, in the other on understanding. On the one hand, they encourage the fear that rivalry will lead to total war; on the other, they take pains to suggest that the tacit agreement will be transformed into an assured peace. The difference is real if one considers the psychology of peoples and the words of their leaders. It is insignificant if one sticks to the basic realities. One must passionately hope that the rivalry of the great powers will not lead to total war, but it is not certain that complete agreement would be preferable to rivalry. Men and states have always feared the hegemony of a single power. Would the hegemony of two be much better? Let us suppose that the Big Three directory which Roosevelt dreamed of, and which was merely a duumvirate in disguise, had lasted: would justice have been better preserved? In any case, a great-power directory would have reduced even further the freedom of maneuver and the autonomy of the small powers. The Cold War cut Germany in two, but the Grand

Alliance had destroyed its very existence as a state. It is the Cold War which has restored to nations of the second rank a diplomatic role out of proportion to their resources. If and when the United States and the Soviet Union can or wish to come to an understanding, their representatives will confer alone without bothering about the fiction of equality between allies.

Is the division of the world into spheres of influence preferable to the rivalry of the Cold War or peaceful coexistence? The question is purely speculative, since the rivalry springs from the universality to which the official Soviet ideology lays claim and from the arbitrary lines of the frontiers between the two worlds. Whatever the meaning one ascribes to the Anglo-Russian agreements on the division of influence in Eastern Europe vaguely concluded in Moscow at the end of 1943 and repudiated by Roosevelt, world partition would have failed as the Russo-American directory has failed, and for the same reason. The rulers of Russia, in so far as they remain true to their faith, cannot *definitively* abandon any nation to capitalist exploitation. The West would deny its principles by recognizing as *definitive* the Sovietization of Eastern Europe. Would a world in which the Big Two had guaranteed the frontiers which separate their respective zones be greatly superior, politically and morally, to the world as it is? In this dream world, would Communist parties still be banned in the West? Would the West have to proclaim that the order which reigns in Warsaw represents the wishes of the Polish people?

Let us return to the real world. Incapable of reaching complete agreement, determined not to engage in a struggle to the death (atom bombs strengthen this determination if they do not actually create it: how much less likely is a Russo-American war than was the Peloponnesian War!), the Big Two neutralize each other and by this very fact restore some independence

to other states. In balancing one another through dis-
agreement, they themselves provoke the neutralities
which they alternately welcome and denounce.

Nothing is more characteristic of this opportunity for
neutrality than the Yugoslav adventure. Excommuni-
cated by Stalin, who naïvely relied on the resolutions
of the Cominform to demolish the walls of the dissident
state, subjected to a Soviet blockade but determined
(and condemned) to maintain a single-party regime,
Tito's Yugoslavia would have been friendless and help-
less had not the deserter from one camp automatically
been welcome in the other. There is a sense in which
Tito was more valuable from the West's viewpoint because he remained true to his faith. Did he not offer a
living proof to the Communist elite of the other satellite countries that they could survive a break with
Moscow? A state which declared itself Communist but
not subject to the Soviet bloc represented in the long
run the most dangerous heresy for Moscow, since it rejected the very principle of the Communist empire,
namely the primacy of the Russian Bolshevik party.
Its immediate effect was to seal the fate of the Greek
guerillas and to restore the Western position in the
eastern Mediterranean.

Ideological considerations apart, a bipolar structure
guarantees, so to speak, the freedom of choice of any
state providing it is favored by geography. The balance of power, the existence of another big power,
tends to prohibit the use of military means against a
dissident state. Would the invasion of Yugoslavia by
the satellite armies have provoked a European war, a
world war? No one knows, no one will ever know. The
masters of the Kremlin would in any case have hesitated to bring a heretic state back to the fold by fire
and sword. The essential fact remains: in certain areas
at least, neither of the two great powers will dare to

employ its armies against a small recalcitrant state, *because the other great power exists.*

The banal notion that the bipolar structure involves the formation of two blocs is first of all attributable to the situation of Europe after the war. This was characterized not so much by the concentration of power in two states as by a "power vacuum" in which the armies of the peripheral states came into direct contact with one another. Berlin, divided between the two camps, constituted a sort of island in the Soviet ocean. The countries west of the Iron Curtain, almost defenseless and torn by the memory of their struggles, felt the double need to perpetuate the American guarantee and to secure themselves against their own discords. Thus the hegemony exercised by Moscow over the countries of Eastern Europe determined first of all the establishment of the Atlantic Alliance and then, as a result of the Korean campaign, the constitution of NATO.

Would the whole of Western Europe have been able to remain neutral, taking advantage of the protection offered by the United States in its own interest? Let us set moral considerations aside, since they have nothing to do with the case. It is difficult if not impossible to have no preference in the choice between a Soviet-type regime and a pluralist one. But there is no obligation or necessity to take sides on the diplomatic level for one or the other, or to proclaim that the one represents good and the other evil. Historically, no regime is ever entirely without vice, none without some virtue (although the degree of virtue and vice is, of course, not equal).

The real problem of neutrality was different: could Western Europe maintain the fiction of neutrality when Eastern Europe, bound hand and foot, proclaimed its attachment to the Slav "liberator"? Could France, which inevitably served as base for the American troops stationed in Western Germany, declare itself exempt from the rivalry in which the whole of Europe was at stake? It is not altogether inconceivable that Europe may one day be in a position to declare itself neutral between the Big Two, that is, make use of the balance of power between them to reserve to itself as large an autonomy as possible. In 1949, at the time of the Berlin blockade, when neither Western Germany nor France nor Great Britain possessed an army worthy of the name, the *diplomatic* conception of European neutrality was simply absurd.

On the other hand, once the Atlantic Alliance was constituted, there was nothing to prevent certain solidly armed countries on the strategic side lines from remaining outside the military groupings. They gambled on the chance of being spared by the third holocaust as they had been by the first two.

What Sweden and Switzerland have been able to do in Europe, where any war that broke out would almost inevitably be a general one, the countries of the Near East, of Asia, of Africa, and perhaps of South America are in a position to do *a fortiori*. Each in its way can declare itself neutral and translate its neutrality into actions.

In Asia, since the victory of Communism in China and the breakup of the European empires, it would be futile to look for two clear-cut blocs. True, the dominant forces on the military level are those of the Sino-Russian alliance on the one hand and of the United States and their allies on the other. But there is today no "Asian diplomatic concert" any more than there was in the past. It was *inside* Japan, China, and India— vast conglomerations, each constituting a civilization rather than a nation—that rivalries sometimes developed comparable to those which have characterized the relations between European states through the centuries. Apart from the conflicts between the Chinese states and between the Japanese principalities, the wars were either marginal (concerning territories bordering on one of the empires—Korea, Tonkin, Turkestan, Tibet) or launched by "barbarians" who, from Afghanistan, invaded India, or, from Mongolia and Manchuria, conquered the throne of China.

Today we are witnessing a restoration of the diplomatic tradition of Asia, interrupted for a century by China's weakness, Japan's strength, and the West's influence. These three circumstances were related: the speed with which the Japanese aristocracy assimilated Western technology and the Chinese intellectuals' resistance to reform represented two different attitudes toward the same fact, the West's technical superiority which was making its presence felt in Asia.

The half century of Japanese imperialism is an interlude in Asia's history. Even today it is very difficult to explain the sudden transition from the voluntary isolation of the Tokugawa period to the desire for conquest which culminated in the dream of the "Asian coprosperity sphere." How and why did the aristocracy whose ideal for two centuries had been the maintenance of an immutable order in which nothing, not even the number of inhabitants, must change, suddenly presume to dominate both the Asian continent and the islands of Southeast Asia? The head start made on the road to Westernization gave Japan an unprecedented superiority, the precariousness of which may well have been sensed by the country's rulers. The West suddenly became the model, as China had been in the past, and imperialism seemed part of the essence of the West. To enter the exclusive club of the world's masters, one must possess colonies as well as divisions, battleships, and guns. Colonies, fifty years ago, were the evidence and hallmark of greatness. Finally, the nobility, whose quarrels had for centuries kept Japan steeped in blood until the Shogunate compelled them to make peace, played a decisive role in the country's modernization. Thus, as in Germany, industrial civilization was introduced in a social context whose values were aristocratic rather than bourgeois. Industry offered the will to power and glory an incomparable means.

The interval of Japanese supremacy might well have lasted a few centuries instead of a few decades had not the Japanese rulers, carried away by *hubris,* set themselves objectives that were manifestly unattainable. A political and economic hegemony unaccompanied by military occupation might not have made a conflict with the United States inevitable. To wage war simultaneously against the Anglo-Saxons and the Chinese was clearly insane, in spite of the favorable circumstances created by the conflict with the Third Reich.

A partly industrialized China has nothing further to fear from Japanese imperialism, nor need Japan fear a Chinese invasion. China's neighbors have always been frightened by the overflow of emigrants from the Middle Kingdom—peasants who take possession of the soil, traders or artisans who gradually dominate the economic life of the country in which they settle. The Japanese islands are already overpopulated: Chinese peasants or businessmen would find no room there and would not enjoy living there. China having recovered its strength with its unity, and Japan having once more become an insular power, the two countries may clash locally within the Asian framework: they no longer have any motive for a death struggle.

The ideological and power rivalry between East and West has altered the traditional Asian setup without making it entirely unrecognizable. Japan disarmed would be at the mercy of the Sino-Russians, were it not protected by the American alliance. Korea, the buffer between Japan and China, is today divided into two states, each of which is attached to one of the great power blocs: in the age of ideological warfare, partition is the substitute for neutrality.

But the situation is by no means stabilized. In accordance with its old habit of suddenly switching from one extreme to the other, Japan, the conquering hero of yesterday, has sworn never to fight again—to be the first on the royal road to peace since it could not be first on the road to war. Japan must accept the presence of American troops and live without means of defending itself or attempting to rearm. The country chooses to keep the American bases on her soil, but even those who make the choice rail against the consequences and expose themselves to the abuse both of the pacifists and the nationalists, the latter aspiring to a genuine rearmament, the former to the resolute application of the doctrine of "non-defense."

The substitution of more or less token American contingents for Japanese armed forces which would be scarcely less token is in itself of only minor importance. China (and the same applies to the Soviet Union) has no reason to invade Japan, where she would find no riches either above or below ground. But the American bases have an influence on the trend of Japanese internal politics. Left to herself, Japan might be attracted toward the Soviet bloc by the desire to find a source of raw materials and a market for manufactured products. Economic interdependence would eventually lead to political conversion.

In any case, the diplomatic situation in northeast Asia seems to conform to the logic of tradition and geography, a logic that has been altered but not destroyed by the conflict between the big powers and their ideologies. If the Russians and the Chinese had sacrificed North Korea, one might have said that the atomic weapon had paralyzed Communist action. In fact, the Chinese acted as if the Americans were incapable of destroying within a few hours the noble cities of the Middle Kingdom. They gambled on American reluctance, either from scruple or fear of a world war, to avenge Korean reverses on ancient stones and defenseless men: their gamble paid off.

The military power of the United States does not extend beyond the islands, or at most the neighboring peninsulas. In Southeast Asia the political and ideological rivalry between the United States and the Soviet Union is only one of several factors. The countries which are linked to the United States (the Philippines, Thailand, Pakistan, and South Vietnam) do not constitute a bloc comparable to the Atlantic Alliance. Korea and South Vietnam (which does not belong to SEATO) are linked to the United States because they are halves of countries: immediately confronting a fragment of the Soviet empire, they have the same impulse and the same need to seek support from the leader of the non-Communist universe. The Philippines are willing members of a Western-inspired alliance by reason of the links which bind them to their former American masters, perhaps also because of the exigencies of their island situation. Thailand, with a considerable Chinese minority, feels threatened by infiltration rather than invasion, and the Southeast Asian mutual assistance pact helps the country defend itself against the former rather than the latter. As for Pakistan, it expects from SEATO military aid which might reduce India's superiority rather than protection against a Communist attack, the possibility of which is fairly remote.

None of the considerations which explain and justify the Atlantic Pact—immediate confrontation of the Soviet and American armies, arbitrary demarcation lines, political solidarity of the Atlantic states—is to be found in the Southeast Asian situation. One might, of course, assume a functional analogy: the Atlantic Pact re-

stricts the belligerents in the Cold War to the use of
political weapons alone, and the Southeast Asian pact
might do the same. But the analogy is questiona-
ble. The threat of atomic bombardment in retaliation
against an invasion of Western Europe is taken seriously, but it would be difficult to take it seriously in the
case of Thailand, Laos, or Burma. This might just have
been conceivable if one side enjoyed a monopoly of
atomic weapons. Approximate equality once established, a threat from one of the Big Two would be considered genuine only in two cases: if the issue at stake
were of decisive importance or if a counterthreat from
the other great power were out of the question. In all
other instances, the intervention of the Big Two in the
regional systems will increasingly diminish or be restricted to traditional diplomatic methods. The two-
bloc system would spring up in Southeast Asia if ever
the small countries there came to feel the same way as,
rightly or wrongly, the countries of Western Europe
felt in 1946–47—in other words, if ever China seemed
impatient to surround herself with satellite states.

At present, China is taking pains to give the opposite impression. Setting aside North Korea and Tonkin,
traditional protectorates of the Chinese empire, China
seems to have been more preoccupied since 1953 with
industrial development than with external expansion.
The leaders of Thailand, Burma, Laos, and Indonesia
have to contend with their national Communist parties.
They are perfectly well aware of these parties' links
with Peking or Moscow but they prefer to maintain
good relations with the Communist powers and solemnly subscribe to Mr. Nehru's five principles, as if the
Communist International was compatible with the
principle of non-intervention in the internal affairs of
states.

The mere fact that China shows no immediate in-
clination to expand is enough to make Asian diplo-

macy, the diplomacy which expresses itself in actions and not in world travel and fine speeches, entirely local and non-global. India's real diplomacy is concerned with Kashmir, which is claimed by Pakistan, and in this question Mr. Nehru behaves not as a disciple of Gandhi but as a traditional statesman. He can find plenty of high motives for refusing the plebiscite of which he fears the result. From Washington or Moscow, the conflicts between India and Pakistan, or between Vietnam and Cambodia, are local matters. From Saigon or New Delhi, the United States–Soviet Union rivalry, terribly real when it seems on the point of setting the world on fire, fades into the background as soon as it subsides. The fate of Tonkin affects the Cochin Chinese, just as the fate of the Pakistan Hindus affects the citizens of India and the fate of India's Moslems affects the citizens of Pakistan. As soon as the fear of general war recedes, the states recently promoted to independence—India, Indonesia, Burma —torn between resentment against colonialism and the fear of Communism, prefer neutrality to involvement, a preference which is as understandable and legitimate as the contrary preference of Pakistan or Thailand. The neutrals enjoy American protection gratis. Why should they pay for something which they can have in any case? Since the Americans have a selfish interest in preventing the expansion of Communism, the non-Communist states are entitled to enjoy the benefits of good relations with both camps. On the traditional diplomatic plane, the whole question is to decide whether the advantages of non-involvement outweigh those of alliance. India decides in one direction, Pakistan in the other. If Mr. Nehru had wished, India might have decided in the same direction as Pakistan: the psychology of public opinion as well as that of the Prime Minister himself tended toward neutrality.

In fact, Mr. Nehru should thank heaven that the

Cold War gives him the chance of playing the part he has assumed. If the Big Two reached an understanding, they would rule over the whole of mankind and lessons in morality would be relegated to the primary school.

The structure of the diplomatic situation in the Near East is still different, though it is nearer that of Asia than that of Europe. The Arab countries, like India, are economically linked to the West and morally in revolt against yesterday's masters, who remain rich and powerful. Without the West they would be incapable of exploiting their oil resources and finding buyers for a hundred million tons of "black gold" per year. Whatever the terms of the oil contracts, they appear too favorable to the foreign companies on which the Arabs depend and which they cannot help but detest.

Economic interdependence and political hostility—these two traits characterize not only the relations between the Arabs and the West; in a sense they characterize the relations between the West and all the so-called underdeveloped countries. They are more heavily accentuated in the Middle East than elsewhere and are reinforced by a unique conflict—the conflict between the Arab states and Israel.

The reconstitution of the state of Israel three years after the end of the Second World War is one of the most extraordinary events of this strange epoch. The idea, launched during the First World War, of a Jewish national home in Palestine and the policy of the mandatory power carried the seeds of the 1944–48 crisis, which did not admit of a non-violent solution. The Hitlerite persecutions made the restrictions on immigration more and more intolerable to the Palestine Jews. Arab opposition to immigration grew in proportion as the Jewish minority occupied more land and created more wealth. Finally, neither the partition plan

proposed by the United Nations nor a bi-national federal state was acceptable or accepted at the crucial
moment. The Israeli troops' surprising victory snatched
from the Arab world a fragment of what had been,
twenty centuries ago, the kingdom of Judaea. A million Palestinians who, at their leaders' call, had fled
their houses and their land, remained homeless, work-
less, and irreconcilable.

The Arab grievances against Israel are by no means
imaginary. We need not subscribe to Arnold Toynbee's
view that Hitler's worst crime in posterity's eyes will
be to have driven the Jews to avenge their misfortunes
on innocent Arabs. There is no comparison, even
morally, between the wholesale, cold-blooded execution of six million Jews and the flight of a million
Arabs in the chaos of battle. The Israeli reply ("We
didn't drive them out; they left because their leaders
told them they would soon return as masters") is no
more convincing. Not that this fact is untrue; but the
multinational state being impossible, the Jewish set-
tlers, once they had set their faces against a minority's
thankless fate, were bent on the expulsion of the Arabs.
Born of violence, the state of Israel continues to be
haunted by violence: it lives by its inflexible resolution to resist.

It offers the Arab states, united by religion but
divided by dynastic quarrels and local rivalries, a common adversary, an ideal rallying point. The more
Israel, by the exploitation of its territory, by its population's standard of living, emphasizes the misery of the
Arab masses and the inefficiency of the rulers in neighboring countries, the more these rulers, feudal or military, concentrate against her the resentment of their
unfortunate peoples and the more they refuse the
collaboration which might permit a liquidation of the
unhappy legacy of the 1948 war. It would take another war, other griefs, other ruins, to force Israel to

take back the Palestine refugees. It would take only a few years and a few hundred million dollars to give them a home elsewhere.

When states clash in local conflict, a settlement can result from a compromise negotiated between the parties, or from a peace dictated by one of the victorious parties, or from a decision taken over their heads by one or more of the great powers. In this case compromise is excluded, since the Arab governments deny Israel's existence. The United Nations were incapable of imposing the partition plan before hostilities began. They succeeded in putting an end to hostilities only when, for different reasons, Great Britain and the United States judged a further enlargement of Israeli territory contrary to their interests. This territory is the result of a military victory. The frontiers are as absurd as those which cut Berlin and Germany in two. They have nevertheless proved durable and for the same reason. The global equilibrium–in–rivalry of the great powers prevents them from imposing together a reasonable solution and does not allow one of them to initiate a settlement rejected by one of the parties. The bipolar structure contributes toward the proliferation of such apparently unreasonable situations. The maintenance of the *status quo,* such as it is, whatever it is, is the only outcome when states in conflict neither can nor will agree and the great powers neither can nor will compel them to agree.

As long as the Middle East could be regarded as a Western preserve it might have been conceivable for the British and the Americans to dictate to the Arab states and Israel the terms of a fair peace.[2] They did not even attempt it, convinced that time and habit offered the only hope of a return to reason. They kept the refugees alive without making their aid conditional

[2] The terms of a peace which the Arabs regarded as fair would not have been so from the Israeli viewpoint, and vice versa.

on a permanent settlement of these unfortunates. Now that Soviet influence is growing in Damascus, now that Egyptian troops are equipped with Czech arms, now that the shadow of the global conflict looms over the whole region, each of the big powers calculates its actions in terms of the other's foreseeable reactions. Would not taking Israel's side alienate Arab opinion even more? In this game Soviet diplomacy enjoys advantages which are implicit in an authoritarian regime. The Jews of the Soviet Union do not protest when Mr. Shepilov makes light of Israeli interests, and the Moslems of the Soviet Union remain silent when Czech weapons flow toward Tel Aviv. The representatives of Islam are quite free to express their views in the United States, and five million Jews live there.

The more the United States and the Soviet Union neutralize each other by their simultaneous presence in this region, the more the local forces gain in importance. In the last resort, a country of less than two million inhabitants becomes a factor of major importance in a zone of global importance. That the Soviet Union and the United States have the means of annihilating in a few minutes the 1,600,000 survivors of Judaism concentrated in Palestine represents a truth which is at once incontestable and pointless. Even if there were not two powers capable of doing so they would not do it. Nor could the leaders of the United States stand by and watch the destruction of Israel by an Arab coalition. The United Nations and American prestige would not survive the annihilation of a member state of the international organization supported by American money, a living symbol of the values which the West calls its own.

It is doubtful whether the great powers are capable of preventing Mr. Ben-Gurion, Colonel Nasser, or a petty Arab king from starting a war. It is equally doubtful whether, morally speaking, they could afford not to stop it. A situation in which the great powers put an end to local wars after a certain time is now reflected in frontiers which are identical with the accidental lines of the battle fronts at the moment when the armistice occurs. This same situation leaves a large role for little battalions. The balance of local forces becomes a condition of peace. By a dialectical inversion, in the age of the continent-state, or the intercontinental rocket, and the mass army, a few hundred thousand Jews, survivors of the greatest massacre in modern history, inspired by a national idea confused with the politico-religious idea of ancient Judaism, have conquered for themselves a homeland in a country trampled down the centuries by invaders who did not distinguish between the rights of force and those of faith. . . .

The three typical situations which we have analyzed (Europe, Asia, Middle East) are not the only ones. Should Africa be partitioned tomorrow into independent states, we would see the formation of multifarious diplomatic systems. Local quarrels are inevitably influenced by the global conflict, alternately magnified or curtailed by the intervention, open or implicit, of the great powers. In preventing the limited use of force the international organization sometimes forbids a solution which would be preferable to the *status quo*. Sometimes also it prevents futile and merciless wars (such as those which set Peru against Bolivia, Paraguay against Brazil, Argentina against Uruguay).

At the present time South America, in which Soviet action operates only through local Communist parties, seems to be protected from war by the hegemony of the United States, to which one must concede the negative virtue of preventing futile massacres. The absence of war is not sufficient to suppress violence inside the South American states, nor does it imbue these nations, created by the Spanish and Portuguese conquerors, with the virtues or the vices of Yankee democracy.

IV. Polymorphous Violence

THE unity of the diplomatic field is real in many ways: the great powers have the material means of acting at any point of the globe. Marshal Tito, Mr. Nehru, Colonel Nasser, and the Prime Minister of Burma exchange visits and pledges of "active neutrality"; at the United Nations, the representatives of the states of Asia and America rub shoulders with the representatives of Europe and Africa. Never have so many states of so many different kinds been in regular contact. Never has the fate of each state been affected, or risked being affected, to the extent that it is today by events on the other side of the world. This unity nevertheless permits the different regional systems an autonomy which the global balance of power tends to increase.

The more unified the planet becomes, the less does diplomacy seem to obey the ordinary calculations of force and the more military technique differs from continent to continent and conflict to conflict. It is as though some artistic genius were trying to reunite in a grand finale every method of warfare practiced by men for thousands of years, on the eve of the day when the progress of science condemns the human race to choose between wisdom and death.

Seldom has the map of the world changed as quickly and as visibly as in the course of the last ten years. Atom bombs, supersonic aircraft, super-tanks have not been responsible for these upheavals. Wherever the big battalions, atomic or conventional, were present (in Europe) or engaged (in Korea), the outcome has been the *status quo*. In Europe, horsepower could have revived the era of the great invasions which ended with the defeat of the mounted hordes of Asia. Outside Europe it is "disimperialism" which triumphs, although it might appear on the surface that would-be conquerors have never had at their disposal such an effective instrument for realizing their ambitions.

It will be objected that the famous dictum, "the impotence of victory,"[1] applies to the United States but not to the Soviet Union. The United States was unable to turn its victory to account either in Europe, since it withdrew its troops and permitted its rival the peaceful occupation of the contested territories (Eastern Zone), or in Asia, since it could not or would not exert a decisive influence over the outcome of the Chinese civil war. The Soviet Union, taking advantage of the German and Japanese defeats, brought under its suzerainty a hundred million Europeans and extended the empire of its creed by six hundred million Chinese.

"Disimperialism," the objector will continue, is simply the liberation of the peoples of Asia and Africa from the colonial yoke, and the Europeans withdrew because they were exhausted by their internecine quarrels. Incapable of agreeing on the division of the spoils, they had to give up pillaging. They were not converted to altruism: they no longer had the strength to maintain their domination. The expansion of Communism proves that the age of empires is not over. The disintegration of the European empires recalls the age-old truth that there can be no empire without strength. The American reverses recall the lesson, also an old

[1] A phrase of Hegel's, *"die Ohnmacht des Sieges,"* in *The Philosophy of History,* apropos of Napoleon.

one, that strength without the will to use it, without a motivating idea, is sterile.

Nothing would be more absurd than to seek in our century edifying illustrations of the theme of virtue triumphant. The non-violence of our Indian friends was effective against the British but it did not save the Jews of Europe from extermination and it would not have protected the Poles, Balts, or Central Asians from the Russians or the Germans. It was not non-violence, if we are to believe Mr. Khrushchev, which spared the Ukrainians the rigors of deportation, but their numbers.

Let us have the courage to admit that the fear of war is often the tyrant's opportunity, that the absence of war, that is of open conflict between legally organized political units, is not enough to exclude violence between individuals and groups. Perhaps we shall look back with nostalgia to the days of "conventional" wars when, faced with the horror of guerilla warfare and the atomic holocaust, the peoples of the world submit to a detestable order provided it dispels the agonies of individual insecurity and collective suicide.

Let us try to understand the obscure logic of this polymorphous violence, of these unavowable wars, of these irresistible and futile weapons, of these states which are born without the material means to defend themselves. Let us not make history more coherent than it is, but let us not create a pseudo-paradox by disregarding one of the aspects of its reality.

Ever since the end of the First World War, far-sighted observers have been struck by the contradiction between the war's lessons and the territorial situation created, or rather confirmed, by the Peace Treaty. From 1914–18 it had been progressively discovered that a war kindled by national passions and fed by conscription and industry tended to assume enormous proportions. In Europe, only coalitions possessed resources on the scale of twentieth-century technology. France could not fight without the freedom of the seas, which depended on Great Britain. The latter, in turn, could not dispense with at least the benevolent neutrality of the United States. Doubtless at first this amplification of the conflict was attributable to circumstances which could be considered accidental or transitory: the qualitative superiority of the German army, the stalemate of trench warfare, the resort to the strategy of attrition. The industrial character of the war nevertheless contributed, to quote a famous dictum, toward making the big even bigger and the small even smaller, in other words to widen the gap between first-class and second-class powers. The Versailles convention increased the number of the latter. The partition of the Austro-Hungarian and Turkish empires into multiple states ran counter to the new technique of warfare, which was itself a reflection of the technique of production. States were created which, incapable of military independence, fragmented the vast territory indispensable to their common prosperity.

This new convention, an artificial one, since it failed to correspond with the interests of either Germany or the Soviet Union, did not easily lend itself to peaceful revision. Could the frontiers of Poland, Czechoslovakia, Hungary, or Rumania be modified without putting in doubt the very existence of these states? The great powers were alike incapable of agreeing on the terms of revision and of leaving the small powers to settle their differences by force of arms (the more so since some of these differences opposed a big power to a small one—Poland to Germany). A general conflict was the tragic but not unforeseeable outcome.

Once again peace seemed to endorse a multiplicity of states rather than the unification of vast areas. In

1945 there were almost as many European states as in 1939. Lithuania, Latvia, and Estonia had been erased from the map but Germany was cut in two. Yet this Balkanization is more apparent than real. East of the Iron Curtain, the nations of eastern and central Europe continue to exist, each with its own institutions, but they obey a single overlord state. The countries created in 1918 between Russia and Germany have been integrated first with a German, then with a Russian empire. They have never regained complete independence and have little chance of regaining it in the near future (although the modality of Russian domination must progressively change).

West of the Iron Curtain, the independence of the liberated nations is genuine in the sense that each of them regulates its own internal affairs.[2] It is spurious in the sense that none of them any longer controls its own national defense. The American leaders have neither the capacity nor the desire to organize a formal empire. Nevertheless, American troops are stationed on the marches of the free world from Berlin to Seoul.

The British and French empires, whose "mother countries" were involved in the Western military system, were becoming a sort of anachronism, the remnants of a power which had failed to survive two world wars and which the rise of a new type of state inevitably made somewhat obsolete. What is surprising is not that France, after the defeat of 1940, should have lost her empire, but that the latter should have appeared to survive the shock. Nor is it surprising that

[2] The objection may be raised that such independence does not include the right to convert to Communism. It goes without saying that the Americans do their utmost to prevent a Communist victory in an Atlantic Pact country. They do not refuse to abandon their base in Iceland after an electoral verdict, but one wonders if, in the event of a left-wing majority in Italy or France, they would defend their bases by force. The Russians do not have to face this kind of difficulty.

Great Britain, in spite of the enormous part she played in the victory over Hitlerite Germany, should have granted independence to India, Burma, and Ceylon. Let us consider one aspect of this historic movement: European "disimperialism," politically explicable, has been accompanied by another military revolution, the counterpart of the atomic revolution: the machine gun against the H-bomb, the spontaneous organization of rebels against mechanized armies. At one extreme we have the laboratories in which the war of machines is being prepared; at the other, a few thousand professional revolutionaries agitate the masses and change the map of the world. Between the two, France (and Europe) has lost control of her national defense, incapable of measuring up either to the technology of the atom or the technique of revolt.

Throughout history, military superiority has been essentially due to armaments and organization which, together, reflected the capacity of the state—a capacity for production and a capacity to maintain order. Not that the conquering nations were always superior in respect to cultural values (assuming one could establish a hierarchy of the latter). If the God of Battles presides over the tribunal of history, it is probably "virtue" in the Machiavellian sense that he judges, not morality in the Platonic, Christian, or Kantian sense. We cannot subscribe to Toynbee's optimism and affirm that civilizations have never been destroyed by force. The legion, such as it emerged from the Punic Wars, was not an accidental accomplishment: it was an expression of the Roman Republic. No one has the right to conclude that the destruction of Carthage coincided with the interests of humanity properly understood. We are incapable of imagining how the ancient world would have evolved if it had not been unified by Rome, or if another city had been the architect of this unity.

We will confine ourselves to a proposition that is almost self-evident. The army which, by its organization or its armaments, triumphed on the field of battle belonged to a society whose institutions were seldom inferior to those of the vanquished. When the fury of the barbarian warriors triumphed, all that their victory proved was that their civilized foes had lost the secret of the disciplined action without which cities and empires are prone to collapse.

In the nineteenth century and at the beginning of the twentieth, the superiority of European arms seemed irresistible. In 1900 a small army composed of contingents from several European nations under the command of a German general had little difficulty in reaching Peking. Some years later the Russo-Japanese War, although it may have given the world at large an excessive notion of Japan's strength, nevertheless proved one thing: that the non-European civilizations were capable of adapting themselves to the military techniques which had given the tiny archipelago hegemony over a great part of the planet.

As soon as she had proved herself on the field of battle, Japan was admitted into the club of the great powers. Because she had opened her doors to Western goods and Western ideas and had accomplished her own revolution, she was soon free from the encroachments of European imperialism. The opposition to reform put up by a fraction of the Chinese intellectuals and the political decomposition of the Middle Kingdom prolonged for half a century a "time of troubles" to which the Communist party put an end. In the perspective of Chinese history, Mao Tse-tung is the founder of a new dynasty which, thanks to the Korean War, had occasion to prove itself worthy of the celestial mandate.

Neither China nor Japan had formally lost their independence. To retrieve the position in world diplomacy to which their history entitled them, they had only to borrow from the "barbarians" the instruments of warfare. This transaction involved profound changes which have not yet been completed. Armed forces of the European type required (before the beginning of the atomic age) factories which could mass-produce artillery, shells, and machine guns—the millions of tons of steel devoured by mechanized divisions. They also need, in research departments and airports, the engineers, mechanics, and specialized personnel without whom a modern air force cannot be maintained. In addition, armed forces on the European model are inconceivable without officers who have received a secondary or technical education and soldiers who can read and write. The Japanese reformers of the Meiji era were right in regarding the spread of education as the prime condition of Westernization.[3]

India, in a sense, has never ceased to be a great power: the British army in India dominated a zone extending from the Suez Canal to the frontiers of Afghanistan and Thailand. Britain's weakness after the Second World War, the influence of the United States and the Soviet Union, the popularity of the Congress party, and the campaign of nonco-operation, were enough to convince the Labour government, interpreting a public opinion which believed less and less in the "white man's burden" and which had always acknowledged in principle that the colonizer's duty and ambition must be to make his presence ultimately unnecessary. During the war the British administration had still managed without much difficulty to command

[3] It is curious that the Westerners, whether right- or left-wing, who are so ready to acknowledge their world-wide influence, fail to remember that they have been responsible for spreading the principle of universal primary education.

obedience. The Indian army fought no less gallantly in the Second World War than in the First. The "liberation" was the climax of a process of evolution which was moral as well as material.

It was in China, during the "time of troubles," and in Indochina between 1947 and 1954, that guerilla warfare, the counterpart of organized violence, emerged as one of the century's demiurges on a par with the atom bomb. Every state not only claims a monopoly of internal power but also tends to subject its conflicts with other states to the rules of law and order. The soldier who loots or kills without orders is executed; civilians are forbidden to fire on men in uniform. Fighting between archaic tribes, however different in other ways, is no less organized than the wars of civilized peoples. Guerilla warfare is not the original form of human hostilities, any more than individuals or families necessarily preceded clans.[4] In our time it is due either to the collapse of a social order, to popular reactions provoked by an invasion, to patriotic uprisings, or, finally, to a deliberate decision taken by the leaders of a state or a counter-state.

The measures taken by a revolutionary government against a traditional way of life unleashed in the Vendée a "partisan war" favored by the nature of the terrain. The Napoleonic armies, which lived off the country, forced the Spanish and Russian peasants to take to guerilla warfare, probably because of the food shortage their exactions provoked. The importance of the respective roles played by hunger, hatred of the foreigner, and attachment to the native soil in popular uprisings has never been calculated with any precision.

[4] Historically, states have rarely succeeded in excluding civilians from hostilities. Often, in antiquity, the citizens of defeated cities were put to death or sold as slaves. In the first centuries of our era, the Germanic invasions brought into conflict tribes and peoples rather than armies. War was badly organized, but it was not, spontaneously or systematically, individual.

The bomb throwings, raids, and ambushes, the destruction of civil and military installations *organized* by the Soviet government behind the lines of the German army between 1941 and 1944 and later organized by the Chinese Communist party and the Vietminh over a period of many years, represent an original phenomenon, on a par with the resistance to German occupation in the countries of the West during the Second World War.

All these examples can be seen to have one point in common: the refusal to allow the regular armies a monopoly on war. The civilians, spontaneously or by orders, combat the armies as best they can. In Western Europe the Resistance was not revolutionary (that is to say, in opposition to the established regime) where it was approved or inspired by the legal government in exile. It was semirevolutionary in France, where it opposed Vichy, a government that was semilegal and semiusurping (or "a prisoner of the enemy"). It was not at all revolutionary in the Soviet Union, where it was directed and led by leaders parachuted behind the lines. Guerilla warfare, as such, is a military technique, not a political action.

But this military technique (individual attacks, surprise raids by small groups, the evasion of pitched battle) is admirably suited to revolutionary action. It is pre-eminently the instrument of "the war of liberation." Even when it is legal in origin, that is, when the legitimate authority has initiated it, it forces the combatants into illegality. Ukrainian partisans who fought against the German army continued the struggle against the Soviet administration. The Resistance fighters of Western Europe, even in Holland and Belgium, became gradually susceptible to extremist slogans. Guerilla warfare, in the twentieth century, tends to assume a political character, just as revolutionary politics spontaneously turns to guerilla warfare.

In recent times, guerilla warfare alone has never defeated a regular army. The Chinese Communists, even before the Second World War, had built up a conventional army with a base in the northwest provinces which they occupied. First comes the phase of individual attacks, ambushes, and brief forays; this spreads insecurity, gradually wears down the administration, and endeavors to stir up the resentment of the masses against the established power, aiming to shake the loyalty of those (the majority) who trim their sails to the wind. To achieve decisive results this method must be accompanied by the creation of a counteradministration and a counter-state. Such was the case in both China and Vietnam.

In both cases, the Communist victory was promoted by external aid. In 1945, the armies of Mao Tse-tung acquired part of the equipment of the Japanese army of Shantung. The Vietminh divisions were trained in China. In the East as in the West, guerilla war between 1940 and 1945 had only a contributory value. But as an instrument of revolutionary action, it is a force liable to alter the map of the world. In the treatise of a twentieth-century Clausewitz, the Communist theory of revolutionary warfare would figure just as prominently as the theory of nuclear weapons.

First of all we must consider the enormous disproportion between the forces of order and the guerilla forces when the nature of the terrain favors the latter —in Malaya, for example, or in Algeria. Some five thousand Chinese held out for years in forest and jungle against tens of thousands of British soldiers. Three hundred and fifty thousand French soldiers have failed to suppress the Algerian insurrection, although the rebels are said to number no more than fifteen thousand. The conviction has gradually spread in the

West that it is impossible to stamp out guerillas by purely military means.

The contrast between the European conquests of the last century and the successful anti-European revolts in this century inevitably raises many questions. Did prestige as much as force account for yesterday's conquests? Or are today's Europeans reluctant to use methods which once seemed quite normal? The guerilla warfare of the twentieth century is organized, the fighters are led by officers or political commissars who, even when they are not Communists, have received a military training, an intellectual education. The Vietminh proceeded to educate the masses with a zeal worthy of the Meiji reformers. The people of Vietnam or North Africa are perhaps no more hostile to the invaders than they used to be. But the French are less convinced of their right to colonize, the colonized no longer believe in the legitimacy of colonization, and above all the subject peoples now have leaders capable of commanding them (intellectuals who have graduated from our universities, officers, or N.C.O.'s from our army).

The Europeans' loss of prestige, the weakening of the imperialist will of the British and the French, the enthusiasm of a minority inspired by nationalism, Communism, or both, the vague aspiration of the masses to an independence which promises both the foreigner's departure and the beginning of an era of prosperity: all these facts together prepare the ground on which guerilla action eventually triumphs. True, without the possession of a territorial base and the Sino-Japanese War, the Chinese peasants would never have been formed into an army capable of defeating Chiang Kai-shek's divisions. Chinese aid was indispensable to the formation of the six divisions General Giap engaged at Dien Bien Phu. In Malaya, where no help came from outside, the few thousand Communists held out vainly in the jungle; in Algeria the insurgents cannot, even if they succeed in organizing a clandestine counteradministration, throw the French army into the sea.

Insurgents have no need of decisive successes in order to win, whereas colonial powers need total victory —that is to say, the establishment of order and security —a victory that is almost impossible on the military plane. In cities there is no way of preventing a few terrorists from throwing bombs at random.[5] North African fellahs can find refuge in the mountains; in the delta of Tonkin the Vietminh fighter was indistinguishable from a peasant when the French tanks approached. Asian or African guerilla action ultimately triumphs provided it lasts long enough, even without waiting for the last phase of a general counteroffensive. Combined with the propaganda of the Afro-Asian bloc and the support of anticolonialist opinion within European countries, it erodes the will to resist or to dominate what it would be incapable of destroying in a pitched battle.

In Tunisia and Morocco the psychological repercussions of terrorism were out of all proportion to the number of victims. Materially the French were capable of "holding on." To put an end to terrorism there was probably no other solution, apart from blind repression, except negotiation with the nationalists. The British too, at the end of a quasi-victorious struggle against a Communist guerilla force, granted independence to Malaya.

Perhaps counterguerillas are the only answer to guerillas. But European soldiers are not equipped for such warfare in the midst of populations of other races.

[5] Indiscriminate attacks against civilians constitute a particularly horrible form of guerilla warfare, since it does not choose its victims. This urban terrorism is a means of guerilla warfare mainly psychological in effect.

Nothing can eliminate the inferiority of the European in this sort of fighting. Human life has a different value in the West, with its low birth rate, than in countries where fecundity remains the same while medicine and hygiene have reduced mortality. Every French soldier or worker represents an investment of hundreds of thousands if not millions of francs, whereas countless Algerians live on the edge of subsistence, making little or no inroads on the collective resources of the country. On the plane of history, this inequality created by the overlapping of civilizations, weighs more powerfully than the equality of human souls before God.

Guerilla warfare is not a return to anarchy. It is a form of organized combat, although the organization is at the opposite extreme from nuclear war. In the latter, nothing is on the human scale: pilotless planes herald rockets carrying thermonuclear explosives hundreds if not thousands of miles. Guerilla organization, on the other hand, depends constantly on individuals: the resolution of each man, the initiative of a few, the endurance of all, remain decisive. Ambushes which cost the lives of women and children, bombs which kill customers on café terraces, do not represent "a fair fight" any more than saturation bombing. The discipline of clandestine war requires more brutality and terror than that of regular troops. There is always a danger that partisan warfare will degenerate into anarchy, and the revolutionary government, having triumphed through guerilla methods, is condemned for a period to use violence to re-establish order and restore its troops to legality.

The machine gun and the thermonuclear bomb, individual murder and mass slaughter: the two extremes of warfare are now encroaching on the terrain which fifteen years ago seemed the exclusive preserve of regular motorized and mechanized armies. What function remains for those steel monsters that from 1940–45 swept like a whirlwind across the plains of Europe from Brest to Rostov? This is a question for the experts, and we shall not presume to answer it here. The fragmentation of the diplomatic field has a military equivalent in the diversity of wars possible in our time. In the Middle East, Israel and the Arab countries plan a mechanized war comparable to the desert campaigns of Rommel and Montgomery. In North Africa, the Algerians are waging a guerilla war based on the teachings of Communist doctrine. In Europe, East and West face one another under the shadow of the ultimate war —the war of atomic weapons, rockets, and supersonic aircraft. These three types of war, Western in origin, equally presuppose science, industry, and conscription.

For the moment it is impossible to rule out any of them, impossible to shape political units to a single model. If there is normally a correlation between military techniques and the size of political units, three military techniques coexist in our time. Only the technique of 1940–45 condemned, or appeared to condemn, the small power. Guerilla warfare does not require big battalions. The atom bomb will tomorrow be within reach of the so-called second-class states and will narrow the gap between great and small powers, which was originally widened by the discovery of the nuclear weapon.

V. Total Threat and
Graduated Reprisals

Is it conceivable that a general war might not be a total war, might not be waged with every available weapon until one side or the other had won a total victory? One may well doubt it, but it is impossible to doubt that local wars can be limited in the twentieth century, as they often were in the past. The least debatable lesson of the first decade of the atomic age is that a diplomatic incident is no longer enough to prime the guns or set off a chain reaction. The statesmen of today are no wiser than those of yesterday, but they are more conscious of what a third world war would mean. Today's real questions are two: how to prevent the extension of a local conflict; and, supposing a general war breaks out, how to prevent it from assuming apocalyptic proportions.

The wars between China and the United States, between Pakistan and India, between Israel and the Arab states, between Vietminh and France, were all limited wars. They were not even declared and they came to an end with cease fires or armistices, not peace treaties.

The states of Pakistan and India had just been born; neither of them was staking its existence in Kashmir. France was defending in Indochina an imperialist domination for which it no longer had the means and sought to raise an anti-Communist barricade which mattered more to the West as a whole than to itself alone. Israel wanted only to exist, being neither able nor willing to follow up a victory whose suddenness took it by surprise. America on the Korean battlefield was preserving its prestige, its moral authority, the value of its guarantees, which the abandonment of South Korea would have irremediably destroyed. The sole object of a war against China would have been the overthrow of the Communist regime. Would the destruction of Chinese cities have achieved this aim? Even outside the present structure of world politics— the balance of power between the two giants—all these wars had one trait in common—a limited objective and a theater of operations geographically circumscribed. As long as they were recognized by the statesmen of the world for what they were, there was no logical reason why these conflicts should have exceeded their initial framework.

Two circumstances might have enlarged them in the past and run the risk of doing so in the future: the use of weapons that the other side considered incompatible with the limitation of the conflict, and the wish to seize advantages which the enemy could concede only after having fought to the bitter end. In other words, if the United States had used tactical atomic weapons in Korea, or if they had aimed at the unification of the country, what would have happened?

The highly speculative answer one can give to these questions does not in itself concern us. Logically, the Soviet Union ought not to have reacted to the use of atomic artillery by deliberately launching a general war (the Communist doctrine carefully guards against the risk of provocation: the Bolsheviks have never hesitated to retreat rather than give battle at an unfavorable moment). But would the aim of uniting Korea have been compatible with the limitation of the conflict? The answer depends on military considerations which even the experts do not agree about. Probably China would have carried on the fight rather than accept the presence of American troops on the Yalu.

It is not so much the use of a certain weapon, however terrible, which threatens to remove the barriers, as the desire for too grandiose a victory. The firing of the first atomic shell in a local war between two powers, one of which possesses tactical atomic weapons, would not mark the beginning of the holocaust. Even two belligerents could still exchange atomic shells without setting the strategic air forces on the move and unleashing the thermonuclear terror.

This is not naïve optimism. We do not know what would happen if a great power ever resorted to atomic weapons. It seems to me desirable that the Western powers should keep enough traditional weapons to conduct operations in case of need without resorting to nuclear explosives. But it does not seem to me either intellectually right or politically opportune to assert that nothing could stop a total war the moment the atomic taboo was violated. The hope is to convince governments and peoples of the urgency of an agreement on disarmament. But the argument risks having a different and deplorable effect: to encourage statesmen first to inaction, and then to drive them, as soon as inaction becomes out of the question, to abandon all restraint. Wisdom and moderation remain humanity's only hope in the atomic age.

The amplification of a local conflict would result rather from strategic extremism than from extreme weapons. The Peloponnesian War and the 1914–18 war lasted for years until the exhaustion of both sides because rightly or wrongly the chiefs of state regarded a compromise peace as impossible. What was at stake was in the first case the ascendancy of Athens and in the second a German hegemony over Europe. Athens had to defeat Sparta to stabilize her empire. The allies did not believe that they could prevent a German hegemony unless they destroyed the *Wehrmacht*.

Luckily—is this optimism?—the present situation does not lend itself to this sort of "general war." The world diplomatic system, which in the middle of the twentieth century constitutes the equivalent of the system of Greek cities or the system of European nation-states, includes the Soviet Union and the United States of America. Now the big powers in this system have two equally powerful reasons for avoiding an all-out war. The risk of extermination by thermonuclear weapons is immense; and the Soviet-American system is surrounded by two thirds of humanity, in Asia, in the Near East, in Africa, and in South America, which each of the Big Two would like to win over to its side and which neither can govern by means (or threats) of atom bombs. Whether or not it is true (it probably is) that the Russians are secretly anxious about tomorrow's China, the men of the Kremlin, like those of the Capitol, are aware that a total war would not ensure the victor a world hegemony but would certainly weaken all the combatants in relation to the uncommitted and underdeveloped countries.

Logically, the existence of the underdeveloped countries should forbid the Russians and the Americans either to agree or to fight to the death.

A war between the United States and the Soviet Union would be a reflection of the kind of armed forces massed on both sides. And we are daily reminded that these armed forces are atomic. The strategic air force is equipped with thermonuclear bombs. The troops of the Atlantic Alliance constitute merely a protective curtain; they must be numerous enough to prevent a surprise attack and to join battle on such a scale that atomic reprisals become politically possible. Have they the strength to fight back *without* the help of strategic bombing, even if they use tactical atomic weapons?

This classic argument avoids the comparison with poison gas. The comparison is in any case illegitimate, since the chemical weapon was not decisive. None of the belligerents expected to gain substantial advantages from it. At the time of the blitzkrieg, poison gas would if anything have checked the speed of the German advance. Later, thanks to their air superiority, the Anglo-Americans would clearly have gained more from it than the Germans (the latter probably did not know that they possessed a gas which could penetrate British gas masks). The Western allies did not want to take the initiative in using a weapon which they themselves had outlawed.

Once it is accepted that a war between the Soviet bloc and the Atlantic bloc would be an atomic war, a number of questions arise. The first, which the experts are continually debating and which obsesses the general staffs, concerns the conduct of such a war. What would the first phase of the battle consist of?

The current notion envisages a mass attack[1] by the strategic air force on the enemy's towns, a gigantic Pearl Harbor which would be to the Japanese attack on the American base what the H-bomb is to the TNT bomb, in other words several thousand or several million times greater. The idea is in any case rather ambiguous; it should suggest that military installations, not towns, would constitute the chosen targets. In fact the public is little aware of these distinctions: Pearl Harbor evokes the image of bombs falling suddenly from the sky one tranquil morning and spreading destruction and death.

[1] On the eve of the Second World War, the West also expected a massive surprise attack from the air. What actually happened was quite different: the attack took place after long preparation. The element of surprise was nevertheless there, and armed forces and airports were the first targets.

But the experts have, of course, pondered the distinction. Some suggest that atomic weapons will encourage the return to a reasonable conduct of hostilities, sparing civilians and their homes, attacking only airfields and regular units. "No need to bomb the cities" was the headline in enormous letters in an American weekly some years ago. The author of the article sought to demonstrate that war, even atomic war, would not inevitably assume the apocalyptic character which people imagined with such terror.

What would be the use, he said, of razing the enemy's cities to the ground since he could do the same to us? Assuming parity or relative parity in bombing power between the two sides, a general staff with any sense would not begin by launching its bombers on Moscow or Washington but would endeavor to neutralize the enemy coalition's nuclear or thermonuclear power. Since there could be no hope of eliminating the stockpile of weapons, which would in all probability be inaccessible and dispersed, logic should dictate that in the case of a future war the bases—a multiplicity of air bases and not a single naval base—figured first on the list of objectives. Moreover, the belligerent who possessed a mastery of the sky, having put the enemy's air bases and strategic aircraft out of action, would have won a decisive victory. As long as there is no passive defense against atomic weapons, the side which no longer had to fear reprisals would be victorious. It would not even have to carry out its threats: the side without means of retaliation, and therefore without defense, would be forced to capitulate.

Against this reasoning a number of objections have been raised, some more forceful than others:

1. Discrimination is *psychologically* impossible to maintain. The belligerent who senses that he is losing

the aerial battle will stop at nothing and no one. He will make desperate efforts to change the course of fate. In an atomic war, the belligerents are bound to feel that their very existence is at stake. One throws in all one's reserves before lying down to die. Extreme weapons imply extreme issues, and these in their turn preclude rational calculations in the conduct of operations.

2. Discrimination is *politically* impracticable. If the belligerents limited themselves to the tactical as opposed to the strategic use of nuclear weapons, the victim countries would be those which served as the battlefields. In the present situation, Moscow and Washington would be spared, but not Berlin, Frankfurt, and Paris. This sort of limitation—the big powers dealing gently with one another but devastating the territories of their allies—would seem to the Europeans on both sides of the Iron Curtain the culmination of irony and horror.

3. Discrimination is *technically* impossible. Cities would be affected when airports were aimed at. Inaccuracy of aim would be allowed for, and explosives used with a radius of action far greater than the area covered by a military installation. But for this very reason, urban centers would inevitably be hit. In the last war, civilian populations did not always distinguish between saturation bombing and precision bombing, whatever the intentions of the general staff and the air crews. In the war of tomorrow, the confusion of combatants and noncombatants would be the result not of human perversity but of the radius of action of the weapons used.

And there is more. Technological progress invalidates such theories of limited war even before they have been put into effect or properly thought out. The means of transport increase in number[2] as nuclear weapons diminish in size and weight. Fighters or fighter-bombers can carry atom bombs. Should the Western powers have succeeded in destroying the Soviet strategic air force, the United States would be safe but not the European countries. It would mean a return to the first decade of the atomic age, when the Continent risked having to pay the penalty for the damage inflicted by the New World on Holy Russia.

H-bombs and rockets have finally outmoded the conception of a limited war between air forces, not so much for control of the air as for the destruction of the enemy's means of retaliation. By their very power H-bombs make it impossible to discriminate between tactical and strategic uses. Paris will be hardly less devastated if a thermonuclear bomb is aimed at Orly and not Notre Dame. As for rockets, they make nonsense of all attempts to eliminate the means of transport and the take-off bases. The launching sites will be too numerous, too dispersed, and too difficult to pinpoint.

The first two objections are not entirely convincing. True, there is reason to fear a desperate and futile gesture on the part of the country with its back to the wall. The written laws of war can be violated, and the unwritten ones *a fortiori*. If H-bombs were not used, if Moscow and Washington mutually spared one another, the hatred of the Europeans would certainly turn against the Big Two whatever the outcome of the struggle. This hatred would be natural but it would not be very farsighted. Now that nuclear weapons are available in plenty, the Russians and Americans have no need to choose between objectives: they can combine both the tactical and the strategic.

It is not the psychological or political but the tech-

[2] Lighter aircraft can now carry nuclear weapons. Nevertheless, the air forces are too small in numbers to be content with pre-atomic explosives.

nical arguments which seem unanswerable. The thermonuclear bomb is and can only be a weapon of mass destruction. If a hundred intercontinental bombers were alone capable of transporting the H-bomb, a battle involving only air forces and air bases would be conceivable, but even on this hypothesis there would be a great temptation to use the supreme weapon as quickly as possible so as not to be deprived of it. Tomorrow the H-bomb will be combined with rockets whose launching sites, through camouflage and dispersal, will be invulnerable to air attack. Either a defense against rockets will be discovered or the threat of retaliation will be the only protection.

What lesson can one draw from these two analyses, the first of which leads to the proposition: "The horror of total war increases the probability of a limitation of conflicts," while the second can be summed up by the proposition: "The thermonuclear weapon does not allow of limited use, and long-range rockets will make the instruments of retaliation on either side safe from enemy attack"?

Historically speaking, in the present situation, before the perfection of the IRBM and the ICBM, while two (or three) powers alone possess atom bombs and thermonuclear bombs, it is highly probable that there will be no general war, that is a war involving the Soviet-Atlantic system as a whole.

It is useless to try to foresee what would happen if the improbable occurred after all and the Soviet Union and the United States became involved in a direct conflict. It is possible, even probable, that in this eventuality the leaders would not be any more sensible than they were during the first two wars of this century. But there is no reason why one should incite them to madness by telling them in advance that moderation is impossible.

In the event of a massive surprise attack on the

countries of the Atlantic Alliance, the reaction could not be anything but brutal and indiscriminate. But provided that the NATO countries keep their powder dry, in other words their means of retaliation sufficiently strong and sufficiently well protected against surprise attack, this hypothesis is highly improbable. What must be avoided is the generalization of a conflict, and this risk is increased if the Western powers prepare for only one type of war, *the war they do not want to fight,* if they deliberately tie themselves, by a senseless military policy, to the choice between all or nothing, apocalypse or capitulation.

Thus we arrive at the great controversy now raging around what is known as the "graduated deterrent." The thermonuclear weapon, especially now that both sides have it, is destined to prevent war. But can one prevent a minor aggression by threatening excessive reprisals? Should one not adjust the threat to the aggression, in other words graduate the threat? The expression is equivocal because graduation concerns not so much the threat as the actual reprisals. It is not so much the deterrent which should be adjusted as it is the measures to be taken in case the threat fails.

Should the graduation of reprisals be proclaimed in advance? What military policy would make sense of this graduation? To announce a doctrine that one hasn't the means to put into effect would indeed be futile. The doctrine of "threats and graduated reprisals" can only be founded on an appropriate organization.

In fact, this doctrine is already implicitly accepted by the Western world. The American reaction to the Korean aggression was a typical example of graduated reprisals. The "new look," it is true, and the declarations of Mr. John Foster Dulles on "massive retaliation" at a point freely chosen, marked a retreat in relation to

the Korean precedent. But the "new look" terrified the
allies of the United States more than its enemies who,
rightly, refused to believe that the answer to an aggression or a local conflict would involve the bombing,
whether conventional or atomic, of towns situated outside the geographical zone of the aggression or the
conflict. What the United States had not had the courage to do or had had the wisdom not to do when it
possessed a monopoly or a superiority in atomic weapons, it would no longer risk doing now that the other
camp also possessed H-bombs and strategic bombers.
Neither in the Near East nor in Asia are there grounds
for proclaiming the graduation of threats and reprisals.
This graduation is already known. What matters is that
the Western powers should possess enough conventional forces, with or without tactical atomic weapons,
for their eventual adversaries to realize that they cannot be sure of immunity.

Thus it is exclusively in relation to Europe that the
problem of the graduation of threats and reprisals
arises. It is in Europe that the choice between all or
nothing still applies. It is also in Europe that the doctrine is most difficult to apply. Without imperiling their
economies, the Western powers can maintain conventional forces superior to those of the Middle Eastern
states, while imposing caution on the Soviets by the
threat of nuclear retaliation. But what is the use of
creating thirty divisions in Europe if this army is big
enough to weigh heavily on the countries' economies
but not big enough to make possible a non-atomic war
on the old Continent?

The NATO force is the result of two conceptions,
both of which have led to a dead end. The goal was
for the heavy units, armored or motorized, to provide
at least a temporary balance of traditional forces (parity with the Soviet forces permanently mobilized or
stationed outside the frontiers of the Union); these

heavy units, adapted to the use of tactical atomic weapons, should be able, in case of need, to stop an attack from superior Soviet armies. The general staffs added tactical atomic weapons to the equipment of the Atlantic divisions because of the failure to achieve even remotely the figure for heavy units fixed by the experts. Finally, SHAPE introduced strategic bombing into its plans, partly because it did not believe in the distinction between A-bombs and H-bombs, and partly because in the atmosphere of relaxation every country was reducing its military effort. But once it is admitted that a European war is almost bound to be a thermonuclear war, surely the Atlantic armies are uselessly large and costly.

The graduation of reprisals, an obvious principle in the abstract, raises more problems than it answers. Where should the demarcation line be drawn? Between A-bombs, and H-bombs—that is, between the tactical use of atomic weapons and the strategic use of thermonuclear weapons? Is the demarcation line geographic or political rather than technical? In Europe, a traditional war would become atomic and a tactical atomic war would become thermonuclear. Elsewhere, even if atomic artillery were used, a conflict could be limited.

At the present time the essential distinction seems to me to be geographical. Outside Europe, no conflict should lead the great powers into a war of extermination, whatever the weapons employed, because there is no issue which justifies mutual suicide. In Europe, on the other hand, a military conflict would be difficult to limit, by reason of the nature of the battlefield, the character of the armies facing one another, and also the issues at stake.

In Europe, for the moment, it is not so much a question of speculating on the respective merits of the "great deterrent" and of the "graduated deterrent"—

in other words on the respective merits of the thermonuclear threat and graduated reprisals; it is a question
of determining a military policy for the second decade
of the atomic age or the first of the thermonuclear age.
Considered as a unit, the West must possess: (1) nuclear or thermonuclear weapons, fighter and bomber
aircraft, and rockets, at least on a par with similar
weapons and vehicles possessed by the Soviet Union;
(2) heavy units capable, in Europe, of preventing *faits
accomplis* and showing the determination to resort to
the supreme weapon in case of need; (3) heavy units
capable of intervening, with or without the use of tactical atomic weapons, in a local conflict; (4) troops
capable of suppressing guerilla action—as long, at least,
as the Europeans wish to maintain their domination
over certain overseas territories.

How many heavy units are needed in Europe and
what type should they be? If one accepted the logic
of the thermonuclear threat, if one admitted that any
conflict in Europe must be an apocalyptic one, one
could probably reduce the size of both the land and
air forces. Perhaps there is even a contradiction between the Atlantic army of yesterday and what it
should be today. Yesterday it aimed at a certain parity
on land and was equipped for this purpose with tactical
atomic weapons. But the exchange of thermonuclear
bombs would make organized existence behind the
battlefield impossible. Mechanized divisions, even if
they were lightened, would be almost useless, and
atomic artillery would be scarcely more useful than
ordinary artillery.

No one denies that heavy units are necessary. One
cannot leave a country empty and announce that the
first enemy soldier who enters it will be met by thermonuclear bombs launched from several thousand miles
farther East. The question is to know how many divisions one needs and of what type. The number of di-

visions depends on many considerations, more psychological than technical. How many would suffice to convince a possible enemy that the thermonuclear threat was serious? How many would give the Europeans the feeling that they were not at the mercy either of occupation without war or of some lunatic individual who might unleash the holocaust by mistake? What consideration should be given, in spite of all the arguments, to the possibility of a local conflict in Europe? Even Stalin did not attempt to bring Marshal Tito back into the fold at the point of the bayonet. But there are more things on earth than are dreamed of in our philosophy: in certain eventualities, even in Europe, the Western powers would not easily resign themselves to the choice between suicide and inaction.

As regards the type of division, the nonexpert hesitates to formulate an opinion. The American-type division of 1945, a steel monster whose formation and maintenance cost millions and millions of dollars, seems in any case ill-adapted to the foreseeable battle conditions either in Europe or elsewhere. Has the fact that these heavy units have been somewhat lightened and provided with tactical atomic weapons sufficed to adjust them to the needs of the times? Whether one envisages land operations combined with a thermonuclear war (supposing this hypothesis makes any sense) or operations in Europe which would not be liable to set the whole continent on fire, divisions as near as possible to guerilla troops, especially if they were equipped with so-called "defensive" weapons (bazookas, mortars, etc.), would probably be more useful than American-type divisions. If they were not more useful, at least they would have the merit of being less costly and more numerous.

At the time of writing, the news arriving from London and Washington leaves little doubt about the direction in which the two Anglo-Saxon powers are moving. Both the British and the Americans intend not so much to reorganize the structure as to reduce the number of their heavy units. In their new form the latter will be destined not so much to traditional operations in a limited conflict as for a complementary role in a total war. The reactions of the German Chancellor and of a part of French public opinion will probably prevent this doctrine from being carried through to its logical conclusion.

The United States is planning, and will concentrate more and more on planning, the ultimate war, the war which no one will envisage launching in cold blood. Great Britain is following suit and, for reasons of prestige and diplomatic authority, is devoting part of her resources to duplicating the effort of the United States without adding anything to the global forces of the alliance. Soon France in her turn will enter the atomic field. Sheltering behind the thermonuclear line, like the French behind the Maginot Line, the Western powers will see the territories under their control, or merely open to their ideas and their goods, gradually contract and shrivel up like Balzac's *peau de chagrin.*

Colonel Nasser openly defies them. Any band of fanatics is capable of driving them out *because, in their technical calculations, they have forgotten the human element,* which rightly precludes the use of *any* weapon against *any* target in *any* circumstances and which will not accept the assertion of power without authority and of obedience without respect. Bombs cannot restore the European master's lost prestige, nor will they imbue the peoples of Africa and Asia with the spirit of submission.

The technology of the rifle, the cannon, and the warship seemed still human: the expression of an inventive genius, it demanded both from soldiers and from leaders, from top to bottom of the hierarchy, a capacity for command and discipline which has been the secret of collective action down the centuries. Beyond a certain point, technology no longer inspires admiration but horror.

The West as a whole may have to pay dearly for the two bombs dropped on Hiroshima and Nagasaki at a time when Japan was already defeated. Whatever such-and-such an American Secretary may have thought at that time, war does not consist in killing as many men as possible at the smallest cost.

VI. History Slows Down

THE balance between the great powers tends toward the maintenance of the *status quo*, whatever it is, when the two coalitions are directly in contact or when they prevent one of the parties from dictating the terms of a local settlement. Will the thermonuclear balance, in the course of the next few years, continue to crystallize the territorial *status quo* with all its absurdities? Are we too optimistic in taking for granted the impossibility of a thermonuclear war? Are we too pessimistic in despairing of a peaceful solution to conflicts inherited from the Second World War?

In the preceding pages we have spoken of a balance between the great powers. The expression was convenient and in a sense exact, but what was meant was a global politico-military balance. The Soviets had more divisions, whereas the Americans had more atom bombs and more intercontinental bombers. The former were capable of occupying Western Europe, the latter of destroying the Russian cities. Tomorrow the Soviets will have as many strategic bombers, as many rockets, and as many A- or H-bombs as the Americans[1] and they will have kept their superiority in conventional weapons. If the balance existed yesterday, in

[1] Even if they have less the difference will be of no consequence: Why kill the dead or destroy ruined cities twice over?

spite of the Soviet inferiority in weapons of mass destruction and the means of transporting them, will it
not be broken tomorrow in favor of the Soviets?

Until recently, the territory of the United States was
safe from bombing, or in any case less vulnerable than
the territory of the Soviet Union, encircled by the network of American bases. Today Soviet four-engined
bombers are capable of reaching any point in American territory, just as the American B-47 bombers, based
in Europe, Africa, and Asia, and their B-52s, based in
America, are capable of reaching any point in Soviet
territory. This aero-atomic parity is bound to have an
effect.

We have assumed, too hastily perhaps, that both
sides would be capable of annihilating each other.
Would it not be possible for one camp to achieve such
a superiority that the other was paralyzed by the fear
of war, thereby once more raising the danger of "dis-
equilibrium"—with provocation on one side, appease-
ment on the other, until the almost inevitable explosion?

Power, measured in terms of the possibility of a thermonuclear war, depends on four factors: weapons,
means of transport, means of defense, and absorption
capacity, or "taking punishment" in the boxing sense.

As regards weapons, there is unlikely to be any disparity. Further improvements are of course foreseeable: the minimum size of the H-bomb will be reduced,
and perhaps it will become possible to control the explosion in such a way that the risks of radioactive dust
will be eliminated. But the side which has the means to
destroy its enemy without compromising the survival
of the human race or accumulating millions of corpses,
will still have to fear the desperate reactions of a country at bay. The explosive power of the bombs will be
increased even further; but the weapons already in the
possession of the Big Two will suffice to render any sort

of organized social life almost impossible. A decrease in the number of bombs necessary to achieve this result would not yet by itself create a fundamental imbalance.

Could a disparity arise from a combination between improved weapons and improved means of transporting them? Here again the likelihood is small, although it cannot be excluded. At the present time the United States would be in an inferior position if it were suddenly deprived of all the bases it uses in non-American territory, since its bomber force is composed mainly of B-47s. These medium bombers were built with an eye to the existing network of bases. Should the latter be modified, the strategic air force would receive supplementary credits. Since technology allows the Big Two the possibility of maintaining on their own territory bases from which each could strike a mortal blow at the other, there is no reason why one should achieve a decisive advance over the other as regards the means of transporting the nuclear weapon.

The present rocket race complicates the analysis, though without upsetting its basic elements. One cannot, of course, exclude the possibility that one or other of the Big Two may succeed some years before its rival in perfecting the IRBM or the ICBM, but this disparity in time, even if it favored the Soviet Union, would be less catastrophic than the prophets of doom would have us believe. The Russian leaders would probably not know with certainty the respective merits of the capitalist and Communist rockets. But supposing, to take an extreme hypothesis, that Moscow possesses intercontinental rockets and is certain that Washington does not yet possess them, the American strategic air force would still have to be taken into account. The global balance between the destruction capacity of each side would not be seriously compromised by a superiority, inevitably temporary, in one method of transport.

If, however, the Soviet Union alone possessed rocket missiles and had also succeeded in perfecting an effective defense against the American bombers, then a fundamental inequality would indeed have been established. The Soviet Union would be capable of putting its principal rival out of action without itself suffering irreparable damage. Once more, these suppositions, without being absurd, are improbable. The means of defense, fighter aircraft and antibomber rockets, are being perfected. There might be an increased percentage of bombers shot down. But given the number of bombers available and the destructive power of each thermonuclear bomb, it is difficult to believe that the leader of either country could launch a total war in cold blood, even if he counted on an improved defense against enemy bombers and a monopoly of rocket projectiles. The experts would not guarantee the statesmen more than a fifty-fifty chance of preserving the benefits of victory after a thermonuclear war.

Supposing, finally, that one of the belligerents were capable of "taking more punishment" than its rival; supposing that one side could "take" a few bombs and the other a few dozen bombs (the hypothesis is not absurd, since countries vary in size and density of population); a state could achieve a certain superiority if it managed to raise its saturation threshold to a significant degree.

The fact is that even the United States has taken little trouble to organize active or passive defense, to protect civilians or disperse the population. In spite of a press campaign, public opinion has remained indifferent; Congress has hesitated to spend the millions of dollars needed to put into effect a plan of defense against aerial attack drawn up by the experts, and the general staffs have not used every possible means of overcoming the legislators' hesitations. Neither in the United States nor in the Soviet Union does the de-concentration of cities seem to have been seriously broached (the transfer of Soviet industry to the east had been conceived and initiated well before the atom bomb). The two states which take seriously the pos-sibility of an atomic war, whose strategy and military policy are dominated by the nuclear weapon, act in certain respects *as if they themselves did not believe in their own threats.* Never have states accepted such a divorce between war preparations and social organi-zation. Fear of the consequences of a radical decision —to rethink mankind's way of life in the twentieth century—perhaps explains this divorce. "Atomic incre-dulity," if one may coin a phrase, is perhaps the cause of this curious paradox.

The speed of technological progress also contributes to this skepticism. Why spend millions trying to keep the sky clear of enemy bombers if the system of de-fense, semieffective against the aircraft of today, will be entirely ineffective against those of tomorrow? Why bother to increase from 10 to 20 per cent the propor-tion of aircraft shot down if, in any case, enough will get through to devastate the major cities? Perhaps this reasoning is false. In theory the (relative) efficacy of the defense can modify the calculations of those who decide between war and peace even if it does not appreciably affect the outcome of the struggle or the extent of the ruins. In fact, everything suggests that the conviction that "there will be no war" combines with the lack of confidence in the methods of defense, ac-tive or passive, to arouse this curious semirational, semilunatic attitude: we devote so much ingenuity to developing the weapons which will guarantee the ruthless destruction of the enemy that we scarcely bother to ensure for ourselves the slightest chance of survival.

The general staffs must continue to maintain the global balance of armed power and, as far as possible, approximate parity in each weapon and each means of delivery. But it would be wrong to count on the maintenance of Western superiority, both quantitative and qualitative, in *every* weapon and *every* means of delivery. The West is not lost if the Soviet Union, at a given moment, manufactures twice as many four-engined bombers as the United States, or if it perfects a rocket with a longer range than the American rocket immediately available. The global balance is not at the mercy of any partial or temporary disparity. Numerical inferiority matters little, given the capacity to bomb the enemy to the saturation point. It is desirable that the general staffs should not easily resign themselves to any inferiority; it is foolish for the press and public opinion to exaggerate the possible effects of a particular inferiority, forgetting that the diplomatic exploitation of a partial superiority will not be any easier for the Soviet Union than it was for the United States.

Statesmen must not take this global balance between the two camps too much for granted, but observers are entitled to consider it as a future probability.

The coming period—the second decade of the atomic age or the first of the thermonuclear age—will be no less different from its predecessor because of a fact whose significance remains uncertain: the substitution of thermonuclear parity for the atomic superiority of the United States.

Until recently the United States had the capacity to destroy the industrial potential of the Soviet Union, and the latter probably had not (in any case not to the same extent) the capacity to destroy the industrial potential of the United States. Some years ago, people were inclined to think that atomic parity would bring about a neutralization of the weapons of mass destruction and necessitate a return to traditional forms of warfare. The reality has been quite otherwise: the threat of suicide has been substituted for the threat of execution. Is the former as operative as the latter?

Clearly the defense of the atomic line was easy, psychologically speaking, when the threat could be vulgarly translated as: "Halt, or I'll kill you." Today, the free translation of the thermonuclear threat would be: "Halt, or I'll choose mutual suicide rather than lose this city, this province, or these oil wells." One is more inclined to take seriously the man who threatens to kill the thief without endangering his own life than the man who threatens to blow himself and the thief up at the same time.

Is there not a risk that the change from the first formula to the second may eliminate one of the most curious characteristics of the preceding phase? Positions which could not be defended locally enjoyed in a sense a complete security, since they constituted a *casus belli atomici* (provided, of course, that they were of sufficient importance). Wherever the war could only be total, and where the Western threat of reprisals was effective and regarded as such by the other side, there was greater security than in the zones of secondary importance, where the nuclear weapon could only play its role of "deterrent," in other words dissuade a possible aggressor. Japan, too important to be sacrificed, too vulnerable to be defended with conventional weapons, was less in danger than the islands around Formosa whose fortifications were solid and whose garrisons were relatively numerous, but which did not justify the use of the ultimate weapon. Berlin offered a striking example of a position locally indefensible whose symbolic significance guaranteed its

protection by the atomic threat. In the immediate future there will be no change in the situation of the
former German capital. Russian diplomacy insists on
avoiding "adventures" or the appearance of bellicose
intentions. If, tomorrow, Soviet diplomacy reverted
from a phase of "softening-up," coexistence, etc., to a
phase of Cold War, verbal aggressiveness, and eventually military aggression, what would happen in Berlin? Short of the occupation of the Western sectors by
Russian troops, which would represent the most striking provocation and therefore the most improbable,
one can conceive of other possibilities such as the occupation of these sectors by the *Volkspolizei* of the
German People's Republic. Would the West decide on
suicide to prevent this moral defeat? What protects
Berlin is not the Soviet conviction that the Western
powers would prefer death to the abandonment of the
capital, but the doubt which subsists in spite of everything in the minds of the Soviet leaders about the
Western reaction. Even if the odds against his losing
are a thousand to one, the gambler hesitates when it
is his own life which is at stake.

Let us set aside these marginal cases where it is
difficult to ensure the protection of geographically ec-
centric positions from the thermonuclear peril. The
substitution of the thermonuclear threat of suicide for
the atomic threat of execution will in any case involve
some modification of interallied relations. Yesterday
the Europeans feared that the Americans might be too
quick on the trigger and considered themselves more
exposed than their distant and powerful protectors.
Today, things have perhaps not yet moved to the other
extreme.[2] But there seems to be a fairly unquestion-

[2] There is already a joke current in Washington, according to
which an American senator expresses the wish to be in Europe
when war breaks out. Rationally, the Soviets have every interest
in striking first at their true rival, the United States, and not at
Europe, which is more a pawn in the game than a serious enemy.

able equality of risk within the Atlantic Alliance. Once the United States is no longer out of range of Soviet bombers or rockets, it represents the number-one target so long, at least, as it remains the only nuclear power outside the Soviet Union. The latter can have no interest in devastating territory which it might want to occupy and eventually exploit.

The change of attitude already perceptible is not solely attributable to the personality of President Eisenhower or the decline of McCarthyism. European public opinion has never been really convinced of "American warmongering." Soviet propaganda employed simultaneously throughout the world two contradictory arguments: the United States as "imperialists and warmongers," and the United States as a "cardboard tiger." After the Asian experience (if the United States had wanted war, China offered them a unique opportunity in Korea), after the explosion of the H-bomb in the Soviet Union, there was no need of Stalin's death and the thaw in the Cold War to liquidate the campaign against "American militarism." Today the anxiety which haunts the Atlantic Alliance is much more likely to be in the opposite direction. Does the atomic umbrella still exist in the age of parity? In what circumstances would the American leaders bring themselves to take a decision which would involve the destruction of their own cities?

The doubt which troubles the minds of Europeans also affects the Soviets—and in this case it promotes peace by discouraging aggression. No one is sure whether a local attack would provoke the atomic holocaust, but no one is sure of the contrary. Yet the distinction between the case of Berlin and the case of Western Europe as a whole nevertheless remains: in Berlin the Western powers cannot accumulate such military forces that a local operation would assume *physically* vast proportions. The magnitude of a "Berlin incident" would be moral and psychological. The magnitude of a "European incident" could be material as well.

In any case, European experts are now concerned about how to convince the Soviet leaders that, in the event of an aggression in Europe, the American government would be compelled to act. Making atom bombs, if not thermonuclear bombs, available to the Europeans is one step envisaged, not in order to force the recalcitrant Americans to intervene in case of aggression, but to guarantee the efficacy of the threat by leaving no doubt about the solidarity of the Old and the New World.

It is in order to solve this problem—how to dispel from the minds of the Soviet leaders any shadow of doubt about American resolution—that the atomic arming of the European states has been considered.

The British decision to manufacture H-bombs represents, for the Atlantic Alliance as a whole, an unnecessary expense. The same sums spent on traditional armaments would have increased the global power of the alliance. But in taking this step, the British government qualifies for entry into the great-power club, which is no longer limited merely to states that boast of millions of soldiers or dozens of heavy units, but to those who know how to manufacture The Bomb. Is this simply a question of pride and prestige, or a recovery, perhaps more apparent than real, of diplomatic sovereignty, in the traditional sense of the term, which expresses itself by the capacity to choose between peace and war?

Would there be a real change if, in their turn, the states of Western Europe possessed at least A-bombs, if not H-bombs? The American commentators tend to reply in the negative. If, they say, the United States has decided not to intervene, the explosion of a few European atom bombs (for a considerable period of inferior "quality" to Soviet or American A-bombs) will not force it to change its mind. On the other hand, Europe as an atomic power would, in its turn, become a privileged target.

The European commentators tend to argue quite differently. If the Czechs had refused the Munich surrender and resisted aggression, the West, in spite of its reluctance, would have been compelled to fight. Nothing is more consistent with historical precedent than such autonomous action by second-class powers. The "protecting" great power would prefer that the "protected" small power resign itself to the enemy's will; but if the small power refuses to resign itself, the great power must follow it on the path of resistance. In the atomic age, this small-power autonomy[3] is reinforced by the possession of a few non-traditional weapons.

Moreover, it is not so much a question of effectively ensuring this autonomy as of creating such conditions that a possible aggressor is convinced that it exists. The more monstrous war becomes, the more reason there is to fear misunderstanding, since the aggressor will find it more and more difficult to believe that a minor aggression will provoke a major retaliation.[4] If the country directly attacked possesses the weapons which justify the threat, the latter will seem genuine. As for the argument to the effect that atomic armaments will bring Soviet bombs down on the heads of the Europeans, it is on a par with the arguments put forward first by the French and then the German neutralists. The Atlantic armies are equipped with atomic artillery; European airports are the bases for fighters, fighter-bombers and light bombers, all of which are capable of carrying A-bombs, if not H-bombs. Europe would

[3] Whether this autonomy is desirable or not does not concern us here.

[4] Luckily, the more terrifying the retaliation the less likely is an aggressor to risk provoking it.

be no more exposed to Russian attack if she herself owned the atomic shells and bombs which the Americans have stockpiled in Europe.

On the other hand, excessive inequality between the allies, with the United States alone possessing the weapons regarded as decisive, might in the long run endanger the alliance itself. The strong are always inclined to abuse their strength. The more obvious their superiority, the more suspect they become. The disparity would not perhaps be greatly reduced by the general distribution of atomic armaments, but European suspicions and resentments would be diminished.

Beyond these possible or probable changes, one question almost inevitably arises. In the regions of the world covered by the atomic umbrella, the *status quo* has been the rule. Should we conclude from this that diplomacy will continue to be static in Europe during the coming years, as it has been for the last decade?

Even as regards the past, it would be wrong to speak of "immobilism." In the Balkans, the guerilla campaign against the Greek government was supported from the outside until Moscow's condemnation of Tito. The break between the Soviet Union and Yugoslavia proved, if proof were needed, that the absence of war does not mean a politico-diplomatic standstill. The Balkans, it is true, differed from Western Europe in that the armies of the two blocs did not confront one another directly. Yugoslavia was unique among the satellites in having no common frontier with the Soviet Union and being ruled by men who had sprung from the Resistance and had not been brought back in Red army trucks.

Is the diplomatic *status quo* inevitable whenever the troops of the two camps face one another? Formulated in these terms, the proposition is banal and almost obvious. Wherever a frontier is identical with a military demarcation line, it would be almost impossible to alter it peaceably. The more important a frontier, militarily speaking, the smaller the chances of altering it by diplomatic means. The Sovietization of Eastern Europe reinforced Russia's defense against a possible aggression and also extended the zone converted to the new faith. Ideological retreat is no more easily acceptable than military retreat.

On the strategic plane, however, the progress of destruction technology tends rather to reduce the significance of the Soviet conquests. Eastern Europe offers no protection against the thermonuclear bomb, and if one assumes that from now on any war will be a thermonuclear war, the potential of man power, steel, and coal counts for little. A war decided in a few days no longer requires the slow mobilization of resources with an eye to which the enlargement of territory and industrial development was undertaken. In other words, if diplomatic rivalry were determined exclusively by the preparation of hostilities, and if the latter were reduced to the exchange of thermonuclear bombs, the aims of traditional conflicts would lose much of their point. A few million people more or less, a frontier advanced or withdrawn by a few hundred miles, a metallurgical production of fifty or a hundred million tons of steel—these differences would not weigh heavily in the scales of history and in the calculations of statesmen. Unfortunately, real diplomacy is far more complex.

The "calculation of forces" which inspires the will to increase a country's human or industrial potential, to advance its frontier to a river line or a mountain range which would be easy to defend, *relates not to the end but to the means*. A conqueror may appear to aim at power for its own sake; but power is normally directed toward a goal which is not identical with power itself;

it is a means of subjugating men, a means of spreading a civilization or a faith.

Atomic or thermonuclear power is of little help in governing or converting the infidel. People imagine that the state which alone possessed these weapons would be master of the world; they imagine that a third world war would effectively ensure this monopoly for a single state. Personally, more by intuition than by proof, I do not think that this monopoly would guarantee world dominion. Either national states would be preserved, and the leaders of these satellite states would soon be as indifferent to the thermonuclear threat as they are today under the bipolar structure; or proconsuls would be sent by the imperial state to govern the subject peoples, while the ruling class of the "mother country" would be enriched by the best young blood from the surrounding populations. The survival of the empire would depend more on the coherence and integrity of the imperial elite than on the instruments of destruction stockpiled in the arsenals. It is not the gold in the cellars of Fort Knox which forms the basis of America's wealth.

The argument whereby frontiers and industrial potential lose their value—the argument that they would be irrelevant in the event of a thermonuclear war—is still vitiated by two errors. The first, and the less serious, arises from the refusal of statesmen to follow the logic of the theorists through to the end: whatever they may say, they do not exclude the possibility of another type of war. The second arises from a confusion, inspired by a false realism, between the means and the end. Certain positions are only useful in relation to an eventual war: the value of such positions is indeed affected by advances in military technology (straits are no longer considered as important as they were at the beginning of the century). Rival states can more easily reach agreement about contested territories once they no longer envisage a trial of strength. But those who imagine that Poland and Germany will agree about their frontiers because the exact demarcation lines will have no effect on the development of a thermonuclear war forget that arms are forged to determine frontiers and not the other way round.

Though militarily they may lose their value, frontiers remain a political issue of the first importance. It was not in order to increase the efficacy of her defense that the Soviet Union extended the zone of Communism as far as Leipzig and Weimar. It was to expand this zone that she sacrificed the standard of living of one or two generations. At most, one can only hope that the "security" conferred by the thermonuclear weapon may eventually make a political retreat in Europe acceptable to the Soviet leaders.

The Soviet military bases, like those of the West, could be withdrawn without much harm. By the chances of battle, the Anglo-American and Russian armies met somewhere in the middle of Germany. Now, both sides hesitate to leave the Germans of Pankow and Bonn to settle their differences by themselves.

As long as these two Germanies are occupied, the one by Russian troops and the other by American troops, the course of history remains, so to speak, invisible. The diplomatic game is reduced to a minimum. The exchange of ambassadors between Moscow and Bonn can lead to nothing as long as Moscow will make no concessions on the Pankow regime and Bonn no concessions on the link with NATO. In spite of these obstacles, on both sides, changes do take place without resort to arms.

In Europe, the French and the British and sometimes the Americans, express the fear that the Bonn leaders may turn away from the West and, for the sake of unity, conclude an agreement with the men of the Kremlin which would leave them neutral or subject to the influence of the Soviet bloc. The Soviet Union replies to the Atlantic Alliance by maintaining its divisions in Eastern Germany. In order to avoid taking any risks, the Western powers refuse to envisage the withdrawal of Anglo-American troops or even the possibility of a Germany not tied to NATO. In this way, the *status quo* is crystallized.

The return to a diplomacy of movement does not require the disruption either of the global balance of power between the two camps or of thermonuclear parity. It would suffice to forgo the direct confrontation of regular armies, but the dangers of this renunciation would have to be accepted. The question of whether the Western powers should yesterday have accepted or should tomorrow accept these dangers need not concern us here. *Militarily,* the withdrawal of the forces of occupation would cost the West more than it would cost the Communist camp; it is not conceivable before the building up of an army in Western Germany. Beyond that, the decision depends on confidence in the power of democratic ideas, in the resolution of free men, and in the unpopularity of Communism's institutions and leaders.

One often hears about the acceleration of history. Our age also provides examples of a contrary phenomenon. The diplomatic "immobilism" in Europe during the first decade of the atomic age, the crystallization of the military demarcation lines in Korea, in Kashmir, between Israel and the Arab countries, can be explained by the atomic weapon and the global balance of power. How are problems to be settled when neither force nor the threat of force is used? Time is needed, more time than in other periods of history when there was no hesitation about coercing the weak, when the fragmentation of the diplomatic field allowed the full exploitation of a local superiority.

The deceleration of history is not immobilism. The

German Federal Republic bears little resemblance to the three zones of occupation of 1945; the Soviet Union has waged and lost diplomatic battles in Eastern Europe. Germany and someday even Europe as a whole may become reunited without resort to arms or, *a fortiori,* atomic weapons.

Europe is only temporarily, not indefinitely, a continent ruled by machines instead of men.

VII. History Continues

Are the foreseeable developments in the military revolution such as will modify the data of global diplomacy in the atomic age? The advances promised by the experts are: the perfecting of rockets of increasingly longer range, the multiplication of different types of H-bombs as well as A-bombs—some more powerful, others less powerful (along with the elimination of radioactive dust)—and, hypothetically, the discovery of some means of defense against rockets. On the political plane, the decisive change would be the general distribution of atomic armaments—states one after the other joining the atomic club which is today restricted to three members.

The development of H-bombs of different sizes and shapes will have the same effect as in the case of the A-bomb; it will arouse the same controversy about the possibility of using "small" H-bombs without provoking the use of "big" ones. The enrichment of the nuclear arsenal modifies the technological but not the political elements of the problem.

An improvement in antirocket defense would not appear to involve revolutionary consequences. There *are* defenses against bombers or fighter-bombers, but the percentage of aircraft shot down would not prevent devastation. Defense must be complemented by the threat of reprisals, and the latter in turn must be based on resources large enough and well enough dispersed so that the aggressor cannot cherish any hope of impunity.

With the perfecting of long-range rockets, the advantage of attack over defense must increase, but the chance of impunity and the surprise value must diminish. The proportion of rockets intercepted will probably be less than the proportion of bombers shot down. Progress will not appreciably alter the present relationship between fire power and armor plating. On the other hand, it will greatly reinforce the defense by removing any hope of destroying at one blow the enemy's means of retaliation. At the present time, we have reached the point of considering flying airports—that is, maintaining permanently in the air a few strategic bombers in order to prevent a "Pearl Harbor" attack on the bases of the strategic air force. With rocket-launching sites, these precautions would no longer be necessary. A potential aggressor will know that he has no chance of paralyzing his rival or his rivals at one blow.

This advantage, it is true, will be a costly one. The control envisaged today over airports, industrial concentrations, and communication centers would cease to be operative. No sign would reveal in advance that an attack was being prepared. There would be no strictly military preparations. The rocket with a thermonuclear warhead would fall from the sky at supersonic speed without the victim country receiving the slightest warning or even knowing where it came from.

I do not believe that the future will be like this. It was the Korean War which spread anxiety throughout the globe, not the first atomic explosion in the Soviet Union, not the first thermonuclear explosion. It seems that humanity has decided once and for all to live as if the atomic or thermonuclear danger, aerial and ballistic, did not exist. It reacts to political crises as it has always reacted in the past; it pretends to ignore the accumulation of the weapons of destruction. Will the perfecting of intercontinental missiles put an end to this strange security and usher in the age of anxiety? No one could answer with certainty, but, at the risk of seeming naïve, I am inclined to think not. The risks of annihilation will be regarded as normal, just as the risks created by cosmic forces or human violence have always been. Will they be felt to be greater because of the multiplication of the means of attack or less because of the multiplication of the means of reprisal? Everyone can judge in his own way. The probability is that men will continue to oscillate, for no very good reason, between terror and equanimity.

The possession of atomic weapons, no longer by three but by a large number of states, will open a new era. The first states capable of manufacturing atom bombs will be European states (France, Germany, Switzerland, Sweden). The gap between the great and the medium powers will be reduced, and the chance of neutrality will be increased. The United States will be obliged to pay more attention to its allies, and the Europeans will have acquired a weapon which the non-Western peoples do not possess. But let us not fool ourselves: this advantage will be relatively expensive. If the United States had put its weapons at the disposal of the alliance, the Europeans would not have had to spend vast sums of money on acquiring the know-how which the Americans already possessed. They would have been able to devote these sums to the development of the resources of the Atlantic community as a whole. Finally, the atomic weapon will be just as useless to the Europeans in their relations with Africa or the Middle East as it has been to the United States in its relations with the Soviet Union.

This first enlargement of the atomic club will not

perceptibly increase the probability of an explosion. The rulers of Europe will calculate the consequences of their actions more or less as the United States and the Soviet Union have done. However, the more numerous the states equipped with nuclear weapons, the greater the possibility, mathematically, inexorably, of insane decisions, and the further away the prospect of international agreement. How can we expect rival states to agree if allied states cannot bring themselves to share secrets (which are no longer secrets)?

This first stage takes us forward about ten years. Twenty or twenty-five years hence at the latest, the thermonuclear club will also be enlarged and the junior club of the "small atomic powers" will have acquired non-European members. Surely it will take a miracle to prevent so many bombs stocked all over the globe from exploding by themselves! Surely someday there will be a dictator to press the trigger!

Will the atomic-arms race inside the Atlantic Alliance lead the United States and the Soviet Union to take joint measures to prevent the enlargement of the atomic club? One dare not believe it (or fear it). Competition for the allegiance of the uncommitted countries manifests itself by repeated offers from the two great powers (offers of fissile materials, reactors, or know-how). Tomorrow the bombs will be a by-product of the peaceful uses of atomic energy, and every country needs this source of energy. To prevent the manufacture of bombs it would have been necessary for atomic industry to be entirely internationalized from the start. After the initial failure, the logic of which we have shown, events took their course. A partial agreement would have been acceptable only on condition that it did not favor either of the Big Two. Once this condition was realized, it would have been necessary for the experts and the statesmen to be convinced of this equality of sacrifice. The agreement would have had to be technically controllable. A limitation of thermonuclear explosions is not out of the question precisely because it meets these two requirements. A limitation of intercontinental rocket tests, on the other hand, would be difficult to control.

One cannot be certain that the logical development will be carried through to the end and that a century hence every country will possess thermonuclear bombs and intercontinental rockets. Perhaps the Soviet Union and the United States, faced with a common threat, will perceive their common interest to the point of imposing a condominium on mankind. But that would be good luck indeed. It is likely that first the atomic and then the thermonuclear club will expand, and finally the club of the powers equipped with aircraft and rockets capable of guiding the monstrous projectile to any city in the neighboring state. This situation, worse than the preceding one, should not provoke despair, but it should prevent us from indulging in categorical half-truths and oversimplifications. Once more it shows that the only road to wisdom lies in the rejection of all fanaticism.

One fact seems almost certain: the possession of nuclear explosives by the majority of states will make us long for a return to the bipolar system.

Books have been written by the hundreds, ever since men have existed and fought, condemning war and extolling it, seeking to establish its causes, analyzing its various characteristics. It is by no means certain that this mountain of books can teach us much more than a glance at the world today.

The Israelis occupy lands which the Arabs of Palestine regard as theirs. Both are ready to fight to the death, one side to retain possession of its territory, the other to reconquer it; one to defend its state on this very soil chosen by history or providence, the other to

destroy this usurping state which was first encouraged
by the connivance of the mandatory authorities and
then created by force. There is no point in asking who
is right and who is wrong. The Jews and the Arabs
both have a good case. They were unable to set up a
single state or a federal state and they do not want to
accept partition. For the time being the great powers
prevent them from settling their quarrel by force of
arms; left to themselves they would fight.

The Palestinian situation in 1956 is unique—as
unique as the return of the Jews dispersed throughout
the world to the land of their mythical ancestors (the
vast majority of the European Jews do not descend
from the Jews driven out of Palestine but from the
Jewish colonies of the Mediterranean basin or of Europe, that is to say converts to Judaism). But the fact
that the Jews were impelled toward Palestine by hunger, adventure, or the pressure of other "barbarians"
reproduces a basic pattern repeated again and again
throughout history: tribes or peoples clash on a piece
of land which the stronger takes possession of while
the weaker is condemned to disappear, to emigrate, or
to constitute the proletariat of a mixed society. At the
other extreme, the Greece of the fifth century B.C. offers
the example of a war to which the genius of Thucydides has given the grandeur and the purity of an ideal
model, and which has nothing to do with basic needs
and senseless struggles. The consciousness of their
common Hellenism should have saved Athens and
Sparta from a death struggle in which both city-states
were to sacrifice their future, but each felt itself threatened by the other. Athens' power jeopardized the
freedom of the other city-states, and Sparta feared that
if the Athenian thalassocracy continued to expand she
would someday be incapable of preserving her independence. It would have been reasonable to divide
Greece into zones of influence. It would have been

reasonable to conclude a compromise peace. But once the war was launched, it became a necessity stronger than the human will. It dragged men on to mutual destruction, leaving them no other prospect but total victory or irremediable defeat. Both Athenians and Spartans appealed for help from the king of kings against whom a generation earlier they had fought together. The same blind passion that set the Greek city-states at each other's throats divided each of them internally. In most of them there were conflicting parties which inclined toward one side or the other and accused each other of favoring the enemy. Athens had its "warmongers" and its "appeasers"; defeat put the latter into power. In the conquered city-states Athens had given power to the democrats, who, in the eyes of their opponents, were no less collaborationist than were the "pacifists" of the Lacedaemonians in the eyes of the warmongering democrats.

All this has its bearing on the contemporary world. No more than the Greek city-states were the European states of 1914 condemned to tear each other to pieces. By all rational calculations they had more interests in common than otherwise. None of them really wanted to destroy the other. It was discovered after the event that Pan-Germanism affected only a fraction of the ruling class of imperial Germany. The latter, as a whole, was ambitious but vacillating, more braggart than conqueror. And yet, as soon as war was declared, both sides had the feeling that everything was at stake. The victory of the Central powers would have given Germany a hegemony that the British were not prepared to allow and it would have put the final seal on the decline of France. A decisive victory over the Central powers required the assistance of extra-European powers. Germany succumbed to the united efforts of the democracies, and Czarism failed to survive the prolongation of hostilities. The war reversed at one blow the trend toward liberalism; twenty years after the victory of the democracies almost the whole of Europe was under authoritarian rule. When the dictators had sparked off the second European war of the century or, if one prefers it, the second phase of the "War of Europe," after a sort of Nician armistice, the nations, this time threatened with destruction or bondage by the Third Reich, had no choice but to fight to the end, ready to ally themselves with anyone and to pay any price to destroy the Hitlerite tyranny. The price was the substitution of a "red" tyranny for the "brown" over half the continent.

Such was, in ancient Greece and modern Europe, war-as-destiny, war which seems to feed on itself, to expand indefinitely, at once mysterious and obvious, impassioned and logical. Whether good or bad, the decisions taken by the protagonists are logically explicable. The events themselves, considered globally, give the impression of having been fated. What is the human meaning of this fatal trend, if not that states prefer death to enslavement and see the threat of enslavement in the ascendancy of a rival?

To explain such wars, whose object seems to be the hegemony of one within a general system traditionally defined as the balance of power between several, none of the explanations such as overpopulation, lack of resources, or economic rivalries will suffice. It may be that Greece suffered from, or had at its disposal, a manpower surplus. It may be that the Greek city-states sought lands or riches outside their boundaries (this was not the case with Sparta). But the most one can say is that circumstances favored the outbreak of hostilities, and for the rest war took charge.

The two main rivals in the 1914–18 war, Germany and Great Britain, were each other's best customers. Never had Europe been so heavily populated; never had its peoples' standard of living been so high. Never had circumstances offered so many means of solving, without a war, the problem of the increasing number of mouths to feed. Never had a peaceful solution been more obviously reasonable and a warlike solution more obviously unreasonable.

Wars for possession of a piece of land or wars for political hegemony seem to preclude the settlements by negotiation or compromise which are always possible whenever the fate of a province or a frontier is the bone of contention, or when dynastic pride or simply the warlike spirit is the source of conflict. There are only two other types of hostilities, if not of wars, which might seem to be equally contrary to the spirit of peace: those which affect the existence of states and the beliefs of their citizens. Rarely has the builder of a state been able to dispense with force in order to quell opposition. No sooner were the rulers of Indonesia independent of Holland than they launched expeditions to subjugate the populations which refused to accept their rule. Massacres and a semiwar accompanied the partition of British India between India and Pakistan. As for the Communist faith, it is, or was, the soul of a sort of permanent crusade, since it proclaims the necessity of the class struggle and equates salvation with the triumph of a single party which does not distinguish between victory and the physical liquidation of its opponents.

Is our century poorer in occasions for conflict over land, over empire, state, or ideology, than earlier periods? No one would be entitled to such a view. Strictly speaking, the case of Palestine will be judged as unique and somewhat anachronistic. There no longer exists on the periphery of civilization the equivalent of the Germanic tribes that invaded the Roman Empire, or the Manchus who conquered China. The Germans and the Manchus were as well armed and sometimes as well organized as the Roman legions or the troops of the sedentary societies of China. Today's "barbarians" need to know the secrets of science and industry before measuring their strength against the peoples of a technological civilization. There are other means of fighting hunger than the seizure of lands already occupied.

With this reservation, which still demands some degree of optimism, the societies of the twentieth century are no different from those of the past as regards the apparent causes of war. Whether it is a question of creating a state, of spreading an idea, or of fighting over an empire, the twentieth century offers an aggregate of past centuries; it does not contain even the rudiments of an advance over them.

Why then do I refuse to listen to the prophets of doom? Why do I reject the dilemma of the optimists who can see no hope beyond a universal state and perpetual peace? My confidence is not based on the single incontestable fact that technology cures the evils of poverty or overpopulation better than plunder and pillage. Certainly warlike or imperialist peoples have often been too numerous in relation to the resources available at the time. An abundance of youthful man power may contribute to the aggressive vitality and the martial spirit of certain societies. Whatever the responsibility one ascribes to these blind forces, it would be equally wrong either to count on economic progress to ensure peace or to fear that the lowering of the death rate will provoke war. Societies are not at the mercy of causes they know nothing about, they are swept along by the current of human passions. These passions have not changed, but diplomatic circumstances and the instruments of warfare are different. This mixture of the old and the new is the world we live in. The pessimist's nightmare is that passions may explode in a war to the death which humanity will not survive. The optimist's dream is that the new circumstances and the new weapons will alter the trend of politics. The present reality is the old game under different forms.

Guerilla warfare is the reprisal of societies or groups which do not possess regular armies or industries or nuclear explosives. Local conflicts with traditional weapons elude the choice between passive acquiescence in aggression or the atomic holocaust. The weapons of mass destruction give the states which are technologically the most advanced a power that they are generally incapable of using.

In every period the technique of war is reflected in the political structure of nations. States are built in the likeness of their armies. But the armies of the twentieth century are as diverse as the methods of warfare and systems of government. In the countries recently promoted to independence, the chiefs of state have been guerilla leaders. In the countries of the West the chiefs of state are those who win the peoples' votes. In countries which are divided between the ballot and the pronunciamiento, party chiefs and army chiefs alternate in power. The revolutionary leaders run the maquis, the parliamentary leaders run the legislature, and the military leaders run the army. The leaders of a revolution, when time has weakened popular enthusiasm and police violence, are as frightened of a move toward army rule as of one toward democratic rule.

The only technicians of war who do not seem to be destined, in our century, for the highest honors are those whom the dreamers once imagined in the front rank: the scientists. In this respect history is wiser than science fiction. Men cannot be ruled by weapons which are not on the human scale. Weapons that are too effective are restricted by the limitations on their possible use. Threatened societies, in the thermonuclear age, will not necessarily be militarist.

The aim of the foregoing analyses has been to understand, not to advise; but certain lessons can be drawn from them.

The United States would have had a better chance of preventing the diffusion of atomic armaments if it had begun by establishing, within the Atlantic Alliance, a genuine community. Starting with the correct assumption that only a Russo-American conflict would unleash the holocaust, the Americans have failed to realize the historical significance which a sharing of the benefits of the industrial and military revolution might have had. In fact, the new weapon and the new industry have made them even more superciliously nationalist. In the vain hope of keeping their secrets from their enemies, they have not even confided in their allies.

Incapable of establishing an empire, the Americans have been equally incapable of rising above a short-sighted nationalism. Even today it would not be too late. By sharing with their allies the weapons themselves, if not the secrets of their manufacture, the United States would avoid the atomic-arms race within the Atlantic Alliance, a race which is bound to have the effect of even further slackening the alliance. Since 1944, American experts, politicians, and commentators have been guilty of a cardinal error. Obsessed with their hopes for an agreement, which was in fact impossible, with the Soviet Union, they have neglected to do what only they could have done—to take an active lead in rising above traditional diplomacy.

Technology does not control technology: only man can control his machines of production or destruction. Those who resent the fact that the harnessing of atomic energy for domestic uses does not once and for all ensure peace between men, those who deride the hankerers after limited war, fall into an old error in believing themselves to be the thinkers of the new age.

The failure of all attempts at disarmament has been attributable to politics. In spite of what they said, statesmen continued to take war for granted. Some countries kept their powder dry in order to defend themselves, others in order to assert their rights or annex *Lebensraum*. Nothing has changed in this respect, despite the atom bomb.

Atomic and thermonuclear weapons, bombers and long-range rockets, make international control alternately easier and more difficult—easier if only the supervision of the factories and the sources of atomic raw materials is involved; more difficult if it is a question of inventorying existing stockpiles. Thermonuclear explosions can be detected by machines, but not intercontinental rocket tests. Aerial photography makes it possible to see what cannot be seen by the naked eye; the possibilities of camouflage increase in proportion.

Finally, technological progress must perpetually disappoint the hopes that are placed in it. It does not provide, thanks to a miraculous and mysterious "gimmick," a guarantee that the enemy has not hidden the decisive weapon at the very moment when he has solemnly promised to outlaw it. Whom can we trust to watch the man we suspect of wanting to kill us? Even if an imperfect control were in fact less dangerous than anarchical competition, states, unless they undergo a change of heart, will prefer the uneasy security offered by the capacity for reprisals to a security based on international agreement, which would necessarily be favorable to authoritarian regimes.

Between the two theses which we posited at the start: *to preserve peace by the threat of an increasingly horrible war, or to distinguish as much as possible between the different types of war, in order to limit violence, I have no doubt that the second is right and the first fatal.* To approach human affairs in the spirit of geometry is catastrophic. To believe that if every war is thermonuclear there will be no more wars is simply insane. Such an idea is obviously impracticable. (One does not defend the Suez Canal Company with nuclear explosives.) If it were taken seriously, it would rapidly lead to just what we want to avoid, since rival states and rival blocs clash at too many points throughout the world. Between peaceful discussion and mutual annihilation there must be other alternatives. Fortunately there still are, in spite of the physicists who have suddenly become aware of their responsibilities, though without acquiring a sense of history.

All civilizations—the Greek city-states no less than the Italian cities of the Renaissance, the Hellenistic states no less than the nation-states of Europe, Assyria no less than Japan or Germany—have had the same task: to limit violence. The methods employed have been different: empire is one, the polite wars of the eighteenth century another. The method of the second half of the twentieth century is *the differentiation between types of war.*

The modalities of this differentiation vary in their turn according to the dictates of technological progress and political circumstance. Differentiation in terms of belligerents is, for the moment, easy since only three powers possess the awful weapon. The United States showed in Korea that atomic powers can, in certain cases, wage a non-atomic war. Geographical differentiation introduced itself automatically. And perhaps it is, or will be, possible to effect a distinction between the tactical and the strategic uses of certain atomic weapons.

The great thing is to avoid crystallizing a distinction determined by temporary circumstances into a basic distinction. At the present time it is impossible not to use the threat of thermonuclear war in certain cases.

But it would be wrong to believe that as the weapons and the means of transporting them improve the thermonuclear threat will be used more widely. On the contrary, in all probability it will be used less frequently. The areas covered by this threat are, so to speak, neutralized, but they cannot be indefinitely extended.

The victors have always had the means of destroying the vanquished. Sometimes they have done so. Carthage was destroyed; the inhabitants of the city which had made Rome tremble were put to death or sold as slaves. The peril of annihilation, which we date from the beginning of the atomic era, actually represents a return to the past.[1] Perhaps the awareness of this peril is newer than the peril itself. Man is by nature capable of killing his fellow men. When there is a balance of power there is also a risk of mutual suicide. Why should the belligerents not learn to avoid mutual annihilation just as the victors learned to spare the vanquished?

There is some justice in the answer that there is a difference between these two cases. The victor, while sparing his victim, nevertheless imposes his will. He sacrifices nothing by curbing his murderous instinct. On the other hand, a limitation of violence during a war limits the extent of the victory. Short of employing the decisive weapons, it would be impossible to force the enemy to surrender. Such wisdom as this would surely open a new phase in the world's history.

There, in effect, the novelty seems to lie. Is it revolutionary? It would appear so. Will humanity learn not to use all its weapons? One hopes so. What other prospect do we have?

[1] Unless the peril of annihilation henceforth involves the whole of humanity, thermonuclear explosions making the planet uninhabitable.

I have no doubt that both the pessimists and the optimists will join in denouncing this interpretation of reality. A temporary respite, both will say. My reply will be no more categorical at the end of this analysis than at the beginning. It is true that the reprieve which we seem to have been granted depends on a refusal on the part of the two great powers to wage the kind of war I have described as war-as-destiny—a war of which the only outcome would be one side's total victory, its hegemony over a sphere of civilization, perhaps over the whole of humanity. Tomorrow the reprieve will depend on a similar moderation on the part of future members of the atomic and thermonuclear club. Nothing can protect us from the possible folly of the kind of despot whom mass civilizations are liable to produce. It would be naïve to affirm that atom bombs were used for the first and last time at Hiroshima and Nagasaki. It would be no less naïve to affirm that every war will henceforth be atomic, that violence will disappear or will provoke the annihilation of the species.

Neither men themselves, more concerned as they are with freedom than survival, nor human societies, striving against each other to maintain their unity, have changed. The Soviet Union and the United States are not capable of uniting humanity under a universal empire. The chance of this, if it existed in 1945, has passed. The unity of the planet is manifestly tending to disintegrate. New centers of force, outside the boundaries of the Western and Soviet civilizations, are due to rise. States will succeed in outlawing modern weapons only when they exclude the hypothesis of a general war and not vice versa. The scientists who enjoin us to create the universal state or perish in a monstrous holocaust do not strengthen our will but drive us to despair. Political wisdom can offer no more hopeful prospect than survival through moderation. It is right to denounce moderation's inadequacies, provided one does not make matters worse in trying to improve them. For centuries, the religions of salvation have taught the secret of peace: they have never promised that peace would be accomplished on earth.

Postscript: Ballistic Missiles
and the Balance of Terror

For some years now the experts have been telling us that the next stage in military technique would be concerned with the means of transporting the new weapons, ballistic missiles in particular, which are less vulnerable than bombers (especially strategic bombers) and free from human limitations. No one could reasonably have dismissed the possibility of one of the two great powers taking the lead over the other. That the lead was acquired by the Soviet Union was not, for the layman, foreseeable, but neither was it unthinkable. Thus I discussed briefly above the "general balance of terror" during a phase of one side's temporary superiority in the means of transport. Now that the situation is dominated by the launching of the Russian and American artificial satellites, it is worth analyzing the problem in greater detail.

Let us return to the point of departure: In what circumstances would it be feasible for one camp to launch a thermonuclear war? The answer has not changed. An aggression would make sense only on the assumption of immunity, or at least quasi-immunity, for the aggressor. This hypothesis, in its turn, assumes the destruction by a surprise attack of all, or almost all, the enemy's means of retaliation. Now, contrary to what is generally thought, technological development makes the complete success of such an attack increasingly improbable.

It is true that in the present state of military science, the means of attack increasingly predominate over the means of defense, which will ultimately lead to an ever-growing volume of destruction in the event of total war. But it is not true that the probability of a total, sudden victory has increased. The opposite is true. An aggressor could devastate a vast area of enemy territory in a few hours, but this devastation would be worthless if it left intact the victim country's capacity for reprisals. It is the capacity for reprisals which, in any rational strategy, must constitute the aggressor's target. This target is more and more difficult to reach. Rocket-launching sites are not so vulnerable as airports; atomic submarines equipped with launching sites will be even less so. In other words, the multiplication and the dispersal of the instruments of retaliation reduce the chances and hence the likelihood of a surprise attack.

The prophets of doom should therefore stop predicting the imminent annihilation of the West on the grounds that it is not yet equipped with medium-range missiles while the Soviet Union probably is, or that it will only have medium-range missiles when the Soviet Union has intercontinental ones. Even apart from the argument which demonstrates "the general balance of terror," there are still other reasons why thermonuclear aggression in cold blood is highly improbable. The Soviet leaders have never taken risks comparable to those implicit in such an adventure. True, they have never excluded war between the two blocs from their calculations, but such a war, for them, would mark the end of the long historical interlude preceding the final victory of Communism—would confirm rather than provoke the defeat of the capitalist camp.

This analysis, though valid against the pessimists,

does not exhaust the consequences of the Soviet lead. It is still necessary to study the respective reactions, rational or emotional, of the Soviet leaders, the neutrals, and the Atlantic Allies to the new relationship of forces.

Against the reasoning of the Cassandras (the West will be annihilated or forced to surrender) we can oppose George Kennan's line of reasoning: what does it matter if "they" can now kill us three times instead of only twice? Logically, the second argument seems to me to be the sounder of the two. Does "the relationship of forces" mean anything at all at a time when, in the event of total war, the mobilization of men or economic forces is impossible and the battle would simply consist of horrible and blind destruction?

But there is a flaw in this logic. The fundamental equality of the two camps in confronting the absurdity of total war does not imply an equality of anxiety. The side which holds, or claims to hold, an advantage, however relative, seeks to paralyze its rivals by threatening the extension of minor conflicts. Nothing is more striking in this connection than the contrast between the declarations of Mr. Khrushchev and those of the American leaders concerning limited wars. Now it is Mr. Khrushchev who declares that they are impossible, who brandishes the threat of ballistic missiles, who presents, in short, a new version of "massive retaliation." The notion of "brinkmanship" has changed sides.

Of course, Moscow has no more *intention* than Washington of provoking the extension of conflicts. The point is that the Kremlin has an additional means of imposing the limitation of conflicts—and this favors the party which is locally superior. While the American theorists elaborate ever subtler conceptions to prevent war from turning into mutual suicide, Mr. Khrushchev brutally replies that things will inevitably take the latter course if a belligerent resorts to atomic weapons, or even if the United States interferes.

In any bipolar situation, the countries outside the zone of direct confrontation partly determine their attitude in accordance with their reckoning of the power conflict's probable development. Their choices are as much influenced by the desire to conciliate the victor as by moral or political preferences. Military superiority, whether accidental, temporary, or partial, reinforces one of the permanent factors of power, namely, prestige.

The Atlantic Allies have been even more powerfully affected than the neutrals. The shock would have occurred even if the Soviets had not taken the lead in the field of ballistic missiles. The transition from the phase in which the United States was invulnerable, or substantially less vulnerable than the Soviet Union, to a phase in which both countries are exposed to the same threat could not but arouse doubts and anxieties in Europe. Earlier, I posited an approximate parity of risk. This was to anticipate the course of events. As long as the Soviet Union had no other means of transporting atomic weapons than strategic bombers, the multiplicity, the dispersal, and the proximity to Soviet cities of the American air bases gave the United States an advantage. Globally, the Atlantic community was equally vulnerable because Western Europe was more so—even if the United States was less. Today, or in the near future, the United States itself is, or will be, at least as vulnerable as the Soviet Union. Quite apart from intercontinental missiles, which are probably not yet available in sufficient numbers, medium-range missiles launched from submarines can strike at industrial concentrations up to several hundred miles inland.

As soon as the United States became as vulnerable as the Soviet Union, a problem was bound to arise: how to convince the Russian leaders that the threat of a thermonuclear holocaust was serious. I have discussed this earlier in my essay. The temporary inferiority of the United States and the Atlantic community has created additional difficulties—difficulties, first of all, between the allies.

During the phase when the United States unilaterally wielded the threat of massive retaliation, the Europeans feared, or affected to fear, that the American leaders might be too quick on the trigger. In the new phase of quasi-parity or balance of terror, the Europeans are divided between two contradictory feelings: how to retain the American guarantee, or rather how to convince the Soviet leaders that this guarantee will always be valid and that no aggression will go unpunished, and how to reduce to a minimum the destruction which would result if the explosion occurred nevertheless.

The European neutralists have always thought, not that Europe had no need of American protection, but that this protection could be unilateral and demanded neither the stationing of American troops on the Continent nor even the formula, more fictitious than practical, of mutual security. The neutralist voice was easily suppressed: during the phase when American territory was more or less safe from Soviet attack, the presence of American troops, symbolizing the threat of massive retaliation, assured Europe as much security as was compatible with the nuclear age. Will it be the same in the new phase opened by the perfecting of intermediate-range missiles?

The arguments in favor of Atlantic solidarity are, on the military plane, stronger today than yesterday. The installation of rocket-launching sites in Europe is considered necessary by the experts to redress the balance of terror. Moreover, the more the Soviet camp is, or claims to be, superior, the more important it is, in order to restore the efficacy of the "deterrent," to show the

Russian leaders that the American guarantee is still valid.

Against this reasoning two arguments have been advanced. The first is one which the neutralists have always used: Is there not a chance of being spared in the event of a general war? Since the United States is the only serious enemy, why should the Soviet Union attack Europe if the latter, deprived of offensive weapons, does not constitute a threat? This objection applies to the possibility of the total war which it is the whole object of Western strategy to avoid. There remains the other objection: does not the nuclear arming of Europe finally destroy the hypothesis of the reunification of Germany and the Continent as a whole by the withdrawal of foreign troops? It is at this point of the analysis that one must inevitably refer to George Kennan's Reith Lectures.

In the months or years which will elapse between the installation of the Russian intercontinental rockets and that of the American intercontinental rockets, is it reasonable or possible to abandon the installation of missile-launching sites in the neighborhood of Soviet territory? The question could only be answered with certainty by experts capable of strictly comparing the performances of the missiles available on either side. In spite of everything, the known data make the answer accepted by the soldiers and the statesmen of the Atlantic Alliance at least probable. The progress achieved in defense against bombers (earth-to-air rockets) calls in question the "balance of terror" on the assumption that one side possesses ballistic missiles and the other does not. True, as we have said, the balance of terror does not imply parity in every weapon and every means of delivery. But technically, and in any case psychologically, too pronounced a disparity in a single type of missile would eventually upset the balance.

Since 1945, the United States has always had a geopolitical advantage over the Soviet Union: it had established bases around the whole circumference of the Eurasian land mass, whereas her own territory was situated far from Soviet bases. To those who accused the United States of provocation (how would Washington react if the Soviet Union set up a radar station at an equal distance from the American frontiers to that which separates the American radar station in Turkey from the frontiers of the Union?) it was easy to reply that a maritime power is always called upon to protect countries which feel themselves threatened by the dominant continental power. If Canada or Mexico feared invasion or infiltration, the Soviet Union would have the means of harassing the United States on her very doorstep.

The advantage conferred on the United States by the geopolitical situation has acquired a new significance as a result of the Soviet lead in ballistic missiles. Between 1945 and 1950 the United States possessed atom bombs; the Soviet Union had none; the United States had a strategic air force; its rival (who would have had greater need for one, lacking a ring of bases encircling American territory) had none. So long as the airplane was the only means of transporting The Bomb, parity as regards strategic air forces meant the (relative) superiority of the United States. It would clearly be paradoxical to abandon the system now that for the first time it is intended to re-establish parity rather than to maintain superiority.

Is this temporary necessity (or utility) contrary to the long-term demands of peacemaking? Mr. George Kennan thinks so, because he sees in it the beginning of an alarming process—the diffusion of nuclear armaments. Certainly, if it is accepted that the Soviet

Union, the United States, and Great Britain are and will be the only powers equipped with atomic weapons, the installation of European launching sites, which involves the stockpiling of atomic weapons and some measure of control by the European leaders over the bombs and the means of transporting them, represents a fateful decision, a return to the arms race, and an obstacle to negotiations between the two camps.

In reality, two questions arise: what is the likelihood of an international agreement on the limitation of armaments? And, short of such an agreement, is it possible to limit membership in the atomic club?

To the first question I do not see why today's answer should differ from the one given earlier in the essay. The stockpiles of bombs are "uncontrollable"; the launching sites will be uncontrollable tomorrow in the Soviet Union (it is not impossible to camouflage them); the Russian leaders will never allow international inspectors free passage through their territory. Agreement on suspending the manufacture of fissile materials for military use is globally uncontrollable. The only agreements amenable to some sort of control would be the suspension of thermonuclear tests and a veto on the stationing of bombs and missiles in certain areas. Up to now, agreement on the suspension of tests has met with resistance from both sides: on the Soviet side, even supposing such an agreement were desired, it is certainly not desired to the extent of major concessions on the question of inspection to facilitate it; on the Western side, the American scientific and military staffs are for the most part hostile and demand control guarantees which are not likely to be accepted.

Since a general disarmament agreement is highly improbable—though this does not exclude voluntary reductions in traditional armaments with or without agreement—I doubt whether there is much choice between the extension or the restriction of membership in the atomic club. The capacity to manufacture atom bombs will automatically develop with the progress of atomic industry. France is not far from acquiring this capacity; Germany will arrive at the same stage within a few years if she wants to, as will Sweden and Switzerland. Will the 200 million continental Europeans, a rich, cultivated minority, the heirs of a great past, be indefinitely content with the security provided by the holocaust's shadow cast over their continent by the two superpowers?

The Europeans would leave the monopoly of atomic weapons to the Americans, Russians, and British if they were convinced that the balance of nuclear power was secure in itself and ensured the security of others. But, setting aside the Russian lead in ballistic missiles, a security based on what the Anglo-Saxons call an atomic stalemate is precarious. Yesterday, the certainty of American retaliation held the Soviet armies in check; today it is the unpredictability of the American reaction which fulfills the same function. The more horrible total war becomes, the less seriously the threat of launching it is taken. It is for this reason that the Europeans demand and the Americans agree that atomic weapons should be stockpiled in Europe. Otherwise, who would believe that the leaders of the United States would sacrifice their own cities in order to save West Berlin, Brussels, or even Paris? In other words, what favors the distribution of nuclear weapons to the NATO partners is the doubt as to the efficacy of the "deterrent" at a time of thermonuclear parity.

I do not deny the dangers which would arise from such a distribution of atomic armaments. But what other prospect is there, once disarmament is ruled out? The one proposed by Mr. Kennan: a renunciation of atomic armaments by every state except three, coupled with a decision, in particular on the part of the

European states, to oppose Soviet power by the threat of national resistance, passive or active.

The European "home guard" idea put forward by Mr. Kennan echoes a similar proposal by Commander King-Hall. In the long run, this is perhaps one of the paths to salvation open to humanity. But I do not believe that for the time being the European democracies can or should make the choice thus recommended to them.

The quasi-unanimous hostility of the Hungarian people to the invader did not stop the Russian divisions. Messrs. Khrushchev and Bulganin adapted themselves without too much difficulty to the tiresome business of repression. The events of November–December 1956, in which some of us at first saw the opportunity for a double withdrawal, seem rather to have offered a contrary lesson. Less than ever will Western Europe consent to remain at the mercy of the men of the Kremlin; in their view, such an arrangement would compromise European security west of the Iron Curtain without guaranteeing the liberation of Eastern Europe.

In the imaginary discourse which, after the fashion of Thucydides, Mr. Kennan puts into the mouths of the European leaders, the latter proudly proclaim that the invaders will find no Quislings and will be faced with the inflexible resistance of entire peoples. Such loyal sentiments would make Mr. Khrushchev smile, remembering the recent declarations of loyalty from Messrs. Duclos and Togliatti. Nor would peoples accustomed to a relatively high standard of living engage in guerilla warfare as readily as the starved masses of the underdeveloped countries.

A double evacuation, on the military plane, would favor the Soviet camp: the Russian troops would withdraw a few hundred miles but continue to make their presence felt, whereas the American troops would

cross the ocean and be gone forever. It would mean
the dismantling of a system of local defense which
symbolized the American guarantee and functioned at
least as a "fire alarm." The counterpart of these military disadvantages ought to be the relaxation of the
control exercised by Moscow over Central and Eastern
Europe, but in this connection the Hungarian episode
acquires a tragic significance.

By dubbing the revolt of the Hungarian people a
counterrevolution and ruthlessly suppressing it, the
men of the Kremlin proclaimed, as it were, a new version of the "Holy Alliance" idea—the Soviet Union's
right to oppose "counterrevolution" anywhere within
its sphere of influence, to bring "fraternal support" to
any so-called socialist regime threatened by a popular
uprising. In the event of a withdrawal of troops, would
the Soviet Union maintain, in theory, the right to suppress counterrevolution? There is no guarantee that it
would not, whatever the terms of an eventual agreement.

The intentions of the Communist leaders, in the
present phase, are perfectly clear: the watchword is
the *status quo,* as regards political regimes as well as
military frontiers. Certainly, the Kremlin is favorably
disposed toward the idea of military "disengagement,"
but on condition that it does not affect the status
of Eastern Europe. In this case, military evacuation
would not suffice to bring about the politico-moral reunification which is the West's real goal.

It will be objected that the transformation of the
East European regimes need not involve the sort of
revolution that would justify the intervention of Russian troops. I agree: nothing is easier than to *imagine*
the Kadar regime or the Gomulka regime evolving toward a peaceful and legalistic democracy without giv-
ing Moscow a pretext for restoring the Communist system. But there is another possibility, which is enough

to make the policy of disengagement a highly perilous one. What would the United States do in the event of a new repression in Hungary after the withdrawal of the Russian troops? The Hungarian army would be better able to defend itself than in 1956. Who can say what would happen and what would be the final upshot of a Russian reintervention?

These are not idle rhetorical questions but a fair reflection of the general uncertainty about the consequences of a double evacuation. Both Moscow and Washington, equally bent on avoiding a major war, prefer a situation which is deplorable in itself but stabilized to the unpredictability of the process which a military disengagement would set in motion. In the atomic age ambiguities are considered more dangerous than paradoxes. The partition of Germany is unnatural but it leaves no room for ambiguity. The Middle East, where there are no clear dividing lines, where the armies of the great powers do not confront each other, where none of the protagonists knows exactly what the repercussions of such and such a step would be, is far more dangerous for the peace of Europe, where a hundred million people are deprived of the freedom to choose their institutions but where the dividing line is known and respected.

This situation is not solely attributable to the atom bomb. Whatever the weapons available, Europe would remain divided as long as Moscow was determined to maintain, in the countries situated between the demarcation line and the Russian frontier, regimes modeled on the Soviet regime and submissive to the will of the Kremlin. Atomic weapons crystallize the *status quo,* since any attempt to alter it is liable to unleash the apocalypse. In the absence of weapons of mass destruction, reluctance on the part of the United States and the Soviet Union to start a general war would have the same effect.

In reality, those who advocate a total or partial "disatomization," a total or partial evacuation of Europe, and expect thus to put an end to an unnatural division, are not aiming to eliminate the consequences of atomic weapons; they reason as though these weapons allowed a solution to a problem which would be insoluble if they did not exist. On the basis of pre-1945 military techniques, the possession of a glacis extending up to 200 miles from the Rhine would ensure the Soviet Union an advantage which it would not voluntarily dispense with. On the other hand, if one imagines that the great powers would only fight with thermonuclear bombs transported by stratospheric bombers and ballistic missiles, neither the human and material resources of Eastern Europe nor the few hundred miles of territory count for very much.

Someday, perhaps, this reasoning will be true. It is not true today[1] for two reasons, which constitute the essence of the objections we have just formulated. Assuming the Western powers could withdraw their air bases and launching sites a few hundred miles, they hesitate to do so because the efficacy of the deterrent diminishes as the United States becomes more vulnerable. A territory empty of military forces ceases to be protected by the distant threat of mutual suicide. Moreover, "disatomization" or evacuation would be conducive to the restoration of European unity only on the assumption of the overthrow or evolution of the "people's democracies."[2] And for the moment, with the experience of Hungary behind us, we have no guarantee that Moscow would tolerate this.

---

[1] I need hardly say that, on the diplomatic plane, I am not against negotiations to sound out the intentions of the Soviet leaders.

[2] I am setting aside the hypothesis of a re-establishment of European unity through the Sovietization of the Western democracies, although a Western Europe that was exposed to Russian blackmail would not be entirely safe from subversion.

In the nuclear age as in earlier times, the conditions of a European settlement seem to me to be political rather than technological. Such a settlement presupposes that the Soviet leaders *agree* to a profound transformation of the East European regimes. If ever they did so agree, everything would be possible, whether because of or in spite of H-bombs and ballistic missiles. So long as they do not, agreements through misunderstandings and diplomatic ruses will be dangerous for all concerned.

There is another school of American commentators which is concerned not with the ways and means of finding an agreement between the two blocs but with the relationship between politics and war in the nuclear age.

Retrospectively, the historians consider that the Western allies were wrong to prolong that war of 1914 to the point where Germany was compelled to accept peace terms dictated by her opponents. A compromise peace concluded in 1916 (assuming it to have been possible) would have been preferable to that of 1918, because the revolutionary upheavals in Russia and Central Europe were the source of the Second World War. Similarly, the formula of unconditional surrender seems, looking back, to have been unwise, because the war aims of the Soviet Union were almost as incompatible with Western interests as those of the Third Reich. The historians regret that the Anglo-Saxon armies did not make a landing in the Balkans and that they did not reach Budapest and Berlin before the Russian armies.

In other words, criticism of the strategy which, in the two great wars of the twentieth century, led to a total but barren victory, is based in the one case on the precariousness of the peace imposed by the victors and in the other on the fundamental division among the victors. The problem in the nuclear age is quite different: the very fact of war is feared, because of the extent of the destruction it would entail for all the belligerents. Soldiers and statesmen are equally convinced that a war waged with thermonuclear weapons (unless it were unilateral) would be insane. Many commentators conclude from this that the sole problem is to avoid war. Some American writers think not. In their view, the aim of the West is not simply to avoid war, but to do so without surrendering, without losing vital positions, without allowing the Soviet sphere of influence to expand continuously. What combination of political and military means will prevent total war and allow an effective conduct of diplomacy in the nuclear age? That is the question which Kissinger tried to answer in a widely discussed book.[3]

In its broad outline, the Kissinger thesis does not differ essentially from that expounded in this essay. He too—like the vast majority of commentators—seeks a middle way between peace and the suicide of the human race. He too observes with some anxiety that the peaceful and pacifist West continually brandishes the threat of the apocalypse. He too deplores the fact that the West, by reducing its conventional forces, condemns itself time after time to a choice between capitulation and catastrophe.

Kissinger observes with some bitterness that at the time when it possessed a monopoly of atomic weapons the United States was incapable of using them to attain its ends. China went over to the Soviet camp between 1946 and 1949—that is, when America alone possessed the weapon of mass destruction. The Korean War was fought in vain; it ended in a draw (which represented, psychologically speaking, a limited victory for Communist China) at a time when American territory was entirely secure and Soviet territory en-

[3] *Nuclear Weapons and Foreign Policy* (Harper & Brothers, 1957).

tirely exposed to atomic attack. Kissinger sees the cause of this disparity between military power and political effectiveness in the intellectual errors of the American leaders and defects in military organization. He seems to believe that with new doctrines and administrative reforms American military power could be properly applied to political action.

I doubt if he is right, even as regards the past, much less the present and the future. The outcome of the Chinese civil war was not affected by the relationship of forces between the Big Two. The atom bomb had no influence on events in Asia nor on the minds of Mao Tse-tung or Chiang Kai-shek, not because Washington had no clear conception of how to co-ordinate strategy and diplomacy, but because the political and military support given to Chiang proved insufficient and because the Americans, leaders and led alike, refused to throw in the extra two or three divisions needed for a Korean offensive in 1951 or 1952. The phase of atomic plenty had not yet been reached, and tactical nuclear weapons were not available. It was not unreasonable to assume that the threat of atomic attack would prevent Chinese intervention, but the fact is that Mao's China refused to allow itself to be bluffed and neither the Americans nor (even less) the Europeans were prepared to face the risks implicit in an extension of the conflict outside Korean territory.

In any case, these are retrospective considerations: the threat of massive retaliation is today at least bilateral. It is no longer a matter of achieving the local application of the American global power, but of preventing a possible Soviet superiority from influencing the course of events and of preventing the extension of any local conflict. In the present world situation and in the light of current technological data, the solutions I would favor are diametrically opposed to those of Mr. Kissinger.

The latter suggests, as an intermediate choice between peace and total war in Europe itself, a limited atomic war waged with atomic shells and bombs but not hydrogen bombs. Atomic divisions would maneuver on land as the naval squadrons of the past maneuvered at sea. Neither side would attempt to secure air superiority, neither would attempt to destroy the enemy's means of reprisal or industrial centers. The aim of such an atomic war would be "to prevent the enemy from controlling territory by keeping him from concentrating large bodies of troops in the contested area" (p. 309). I find it difficult to take this hypothesis seriously. The extent of the devastation such a war would inflict on such a highly populated continent as Europe makes it highly improbable in my opinion. The disproportion between the cost of such hostilities and the results they could achieve would be colossal. How convince the enemy that his airports, his launching sites, his cities would be spared? Who would even launch such hostilities unless he was determined to persist to the bitter end? Who would stop the fighting, and how, with neither side having gained a clear-cut victory and the theater of operations completely devastated? The idea of limited atomic war, in Europe at least, seems to me ultimately as improbable as the idea of graduated reprisals (in the sense of limiting reprisals to military objectives).

Does the same apply outside Europe? There I am not so sure. It is obviously impossible to foresee all the various possibilities; we are still groping in the dark world of nuclear diplomacy. For the time being, at least, it seems essential to preserve the possibility of limited wars. Men are incapable of conducting politics without violence and they do not want a general suicide pact. Since, at the moment, only three states possess atomic arms, wars could be waged with traditional weapons, provided the belligerents agreed to limit their objectives and not provoke the intervention of atomic powers.

As for the latter, could they fight each other outside Europe without using atomic weapons? Kissinger doubts whether they could and he puts forward a strong case in favor of his view. A commander would hesitate to deploy his forces as he normally should in the case of a "traditional" battle for fear that his opponent might use tactical atomic weapons. Moreover, the fact that the Soviet and especially the American armies have been adapted to the use of tactical atomic weapons would make a campaign of the Korean type technically difficult.

I do not deny the validity of these arguments but neither do I regard them as overwhelming. Throughout the Korean War, the American general staff gambled on the immunity of the Japanese base, on the non-intervention of Soviet submarines. In the same way, it is not inconceivable that in the event of military operations in the Near East both sides might tacitly agree to exclude atomic weapons. Would one side gain an advantage from such an abstention? Kissinger suggests that the strategy of limited atomic war corresponds most closely with American interests. Atomic weapons would preclude the massive concentration of conventional forces, which is the tactic adopted by the Russians and Chinese in past wars (including the Korean War). And American industry—the economic and social system of the United States—would be better equipped than the Soviets' to produce the diversified and complex weapons required for atomic warfare.

Assuming all this to be true and that a limited atomic war, outside Europe, is in certain circumstances possible, the fact nevertheless remains that the use of atomic weapons increases the risk—if only psychologically—of total war, and that the Western leaders, elected democratically, are almost bound to be at a disadvantage in a military-diplomatic poker game with the leaders of a totalitarian party. The men of the Kremlin have always been convinced that the American leaders would not launch an atomic war except as a last resort (this was true even at the time of America's atomic monopoly). The West, on the other hand—and wrongly perhaps—fears a wild gesture on the part of Moscow. A strategy of limited atomic war, as recommended by Kissinger, presupposes an equality of fear and of nerve between the two camps. Even before the sputniks such equality did not exist, any more than it existed from 1933–39 between Hitler and Chamberlain and Daladier.

Many readers will probably regard these analyses as pessimistic or even devoid of hope. This is not the spirit in which I have written them or the conclusion that I personally draw from them.

A revolution has occurred in military history: thanks to scientific progress, the weapons now available to the strategist are such that the destruction in the event of unlimited war would bear no relation to any politically conceivable objective. In certain circumstances, the quantity of thermonuclear weapons necessary to destroy the putative enemy's means of reprisal would imperil the aggressor country itself and possibly the survival of the entire human race.

In the abstract, the best answer to this unprecedented challenge would be the creation of a single supreme authority over mankind, or at least the creation of a world authority over scientific weapons. But this truth—or truism—is for the time being irrelevant: for reasons which should be obvious to anyone, the differences between the great powers, though they need not lead to a war to the death, preclude a merging of sovereignties or a planetary condominium.

This theoretically ideal solution being out of the

question, the world has provisionally settled for the next-best thing—to keep the threat of total war for certain contingencies and certain areas, and elsewhere to conduct its affairs by means of a traditional diplomacy, restricting as much as possible the use of regular armies and accepting the possibility of wars waged with "anachronistic" weapons—weapons outdated by technological progress. This solution, of course, means gambling on the moderation of the world's statesmen; it presupposes that none of them will make a wild decision or miscalculate their rivals' intentions to the point of making a false move. The gamble necessarily entails some risk, but humanity has always lived dangerously.

Now, at the beginning of 1958, for reasons that are fortunately only temporary, the West has lost some of its equanimity in facing this danger. The Soviets have stolen a march on the West in the field of ballistic missiles. The invulnerability of American territory, which guaranteed the efficacy of the deterrent, is past. The protection of the West's retaliatory capacity requires that a proportion of the American Air Force should be permanently in the air. The threat of massive retaliation has become bilateral. But these vicissitudes of the scientific arms race need to be put into long-term perspective. They do not upset the "general balance of terror"; they do not affect the salient feature of the present phase of history, which is that mankind, *for the first time in its history,* is preparing for a war it does not want to fight and looks to the common sense of statesmen to avoid it.

During this phase, or at least during the first few years of this phase, the new scientific weapons have had only a limited effect on the course of events outside Europe. The Europeans west of the Iron Curtain have grown accustomed to the strange protection afforded by the threat of total war in the event of military operations and, as it were, guaranteed by the direct confrontation of the armies of the Big Two. The presence of the American and Russian armies along the demarcation line is the symbol of the deterrent, and the Europeans have come to believe that any withdrawal of these armies, whether total or partial, would weaken it. In a zone emptied of American troops or atomic weapons, military operations would once more become possible because no one would believe they would provoke thermonuclear retaliation.

But the European stalemate is not necessarily permanent. Someday, perhaps, the Europeans will no longer feel the need for the presence of American troops as a symbol of the deterrent, and the Soviets will no longer insist on politico-ideological conformity from the rulers of Eastern Europe. In themselves, atomic weapons are responsible for neither of these situations. Indeed, in the long run they may render them both unnecessary.

Will the diffusion of atomic weapons increase the world's perils? In certain respects it will certainly create additional risks (irrational decisions by national leaders, for example), but it is for the West to guarantee that the acquisition of these weapons by the European states will be accompanied by a mutually agreed-on system of control. By creating a genuine community among themselves, the Western powers would guard against the future; they would open a middle way between the restriction of membership in the nuclear club, which is impossible of realization, and the dangers of atomic anarchy.

Should one try to penetrate the secrets of the future beyond the present phase of two coalitions armed with all the instruments of destruction which science can offer to human folly? What would be the point, unless to ward off the temptation to despair? Science not only makes wars insane because the havoc caused would be out of all proportion with any conceivable issue at stake; it also eliminates most of the *economic* causes of wars and brings countries together willy-nilly.

The men and the nations sharing the benefits of modern industrial civilization are divided chiefly by ideological prejudices and human passions. The power of false ideas condemns all hope of world unity in the immediate future, but not the hope of a gradual, ultimate reconciliation of the human race.

DATE DUE

GAYLORD			PRINTED IN U.S.A.

IN NORTON PAPERBOUND EDITIONS

ON WAR